CONTENTS

Opening Statements of Members

Witnesses

Submissions for the Record

S. HRG. 109–53

MEDICAL LIABILITY REFORM

HEARING

BEFORE THE

JOINT ECONOMIC COMMITTEE
CONGRESS OF THE UNITED STATES

ONE HUNDRED NINTH CONGRESS

FIRST SESSION

APRIL 28, 2005

Printed for the use of the Joint Economic Committee

U.S. GOVERNMENT PRINTING OFFICE

21–772 PDF WASHINGTON : 2005

For sale by the Superintendent of Documents, U.S. Government Printing Office
Internet: bookstore.gpo.gov Phone: toll free (866) 512–1800; DC area (202) 512–1800
Fax: (202) 512–2250 Mail: Stop SSOP, Washington, DC 20402–0001

JOINT ECONOMIC COMMITTEE

[Created pursuant to Sec. 5(a) of Public Law 304, 79th Congress]

MEDICAL LIABILITY REFORM

THURSDAY, APRIL 28, 2005

UNITED STATES CONGRESS,
JOINT ECONOMIC COMMITTEE,
Washington, DC.

The Committee met, pursuant to notice, at 10:05 a.m., in room 2226, Rayburn House Office Building, the Honorable Jim Saxton, Chairman of the Committee, presiding.

Present: Representatives Saxton, Hinchey, and Cummings. Senator Reed.

Staff present: Chris Frenze, Dan Miller, Brian Higginbotham, Colleen Healy, John Kachtik, Tom Miller, Chad Stone, John McInerney, Daphne Clones Federing, and Nan Gibson.

OPENING STATEMENT OF REPRESENTATIVE JIM SAXTON, CHAIRMAN

Representative Saxton. Good morning, Dr. McClellan. Welcome.

Dr. McClellan. Good morning. Thank you, Mr. Chairman.

Representative Saxton. We will begin the hearing. I would like to make a short statement which emphasizes what I think is the tremendous importance of the subject that we are here to discuss today.

In doing so, it is a pleasure to welcome Dr. Mark McClellan to the Joint Economic Committee. Dr. McClellan brings a wealth of experience and knowledge to bear on the subject of medical liability insurance, tort medical liability reform. Currently, Dr. McClellan serves as Administrator of the Centers for Medicare and Medicaid Services, overseeing approximately one-third of the health care spending of the U.S. In addition to being a board-certified physician of internal medicine, Dr. McClellan is a Ph.D. economist. He has previously served as the Commissioner of the Food and Drug Administration and as a member of President Bush's Council of Economic Advisers.

There is little doubt that our Nation's medical liability laws need reform. Over the past few years, premiums have skyrocketed. In just the last 5 years, total medical liability costs jumped 47 percent to a record high of $27 billion.

I would just like to refer everybody to this chart. Maybe you could turn it so that we can see it here and they can see it in the audience perhaps a little bit better than that.

In looking at this chart this morning, I was absolutely amazed. I knew that medical liability malpractice costs had gone up, but when I looked at this and saw that kind of in the middle, among the middle bars there, there is a $9.2 billion mark; that was 1990. Today, medical malpractice costs are almost $27 billion. So since 1990, medical malpractice costs have actually tripled in just those few years. This is indeed an issue that bears close examination.

One of the central cost drivers is rising claims costs. According to the legal research firm Jury Verdict Research, the median trial award for medical liability claims stands at an incredible $1.2 million, and a recent Department of Justice study reported that nearly two-thirds of medical liability trial awards exceed $250,000.

Here is another chart that shows growth in median liability claims. As recently as 1997, the median liability claim, as represented by the shortest bar to the left of the chart, was $500,000.

Today, as I mentioned a minute ago, the median trial award for medical liability claims stands at an incredible $1.2 million. Once again, just since 1997, these claims have more than doubled. This rise in costs has reached the point where the quality and availability of health care suffer. Faced with premiums increasing 20 to 30 percent a year, many doctors are cutting back on the scope and availability of their services. Nowhere is this trend more apparent than in obstetrics, where numerous OB/GYNs have decided it is just easier to drop OB altogether. Some doctors have elected early retirement or have relocated away from high litigation areas.

Emergency rooms and trauma centers have also been hurt by the current crisis. The threat of lawsuits has made the practice of defensive medicine commonplace, and as a result, patients are subjected to more tests and procedures than may be warranted by clinical factors alone.

Despite the rise in costs, the system is not better at compensating the negligently injured. The typical time that elapses between the date of injury and a verdict is close to 5 years. And, of course, legal fees go on during that period of time.

Moreover, it is widely recognized—and this is an unbelievable fact that we came across in studying this subject a year or so ago—it is widely recognized that only a small fraction of negligently injured patients even file a claim. At the same time, a large majority, around 80 percent, of medical liability claims do not even involve negligent injuries. One study even found that more than half of all medical liability claims do not involve an injury at all.

The shortcomings in the current tort system are such that *The Washington Post* has noted that, and I quote: "The staggering costs of America's civil justice system are unacceptable. The tort system is something of a casino, offering windfall judgments to a small number of claimants and nothing to others—with the merits of cases seeming almost irrelevant to their valuation."

Although each State faces its own set of challenges and problems, the medical liability crisis has nonetheless reached national proportions.

I wonder if we could put the chart up of the map of the U.S. so that I can just point out that some States have taken steps to mitigate the problem. The States in red are represented—this is an American medical liability cost and national view put out by the American Medical Association, just so that everyone knows its source.

But those States that are depicted in red are States that are actually in crisis. I am from New Jersey; it is red. The States that are showing the probability of moving toward crisis are in yellow and States that have stepped up to the bar and have done something about it are actually in white.

I might note that in California—if we can look at the next chart, California is one of the States that did something about this problem. The red line indicates the national statistics and how this problem has exacerbated itself. We see that the increases that start during the 1970s were gradual at first, but as we move forward, the premium growth during the 1990s and now in the 2000s is just shooting upward. Contrast that with what happened in California, which is shown by the blue line.

In the 1970s and 1980s, the costs of premiums for medical liability insurance began to increase. But in 1975, California enacted a cap. We can see that the premium growth stabilized right after that reform occurred, and we have not seen the kind of growth in California that we have seen nationally. So there are solutions apparently to this problem.

[The prepared statement and charts submitted by Representative Saxton appear in the Submissions for the Record on page 29.]

Thus, we want to thank Dr. McClellan for being here today to provide some insight into the problem and the direction of reform. Before we go to Dr. McClellan, we will turn to my friend, Senator Reed——

Senator Reed. Thank you very much.

Representative Saxton [continuing]. ——Whom I might publicly congratulate. He got married last weekend, a great wedding at West Point, I hear.

Senator Reed. For the first time.

OPENING STATEMENT OF SENATOR JACK REED, RANKING MINORITY MEMBER

Senator Reed. Thank you very much, Mr. Chairman, and thank you, Dr. McClellan. Welcome.

On the campaign trail last year, President Bush repeatedly criticized trial lawyers for filing junk lawsuits that he said were responsible for rising health care costs. The centerpiece of the Administration's medical liability reform would cap non-economic damages at $250,000 and institute a 3-year statute of limitations on most lawsuits.

The 2004 Economic Report of the President stated that the President's reform plan would lower the cost of providing health care. However, there is little, if any, evidence to support that claim. Hopefully, Dr. McClellan, you can shed some light on that.

While it is certainly troubling that medical malpractice premiums for doctors have been rising rapidly in recent years and many physicians in my State have informed me of the cost burden and potential impact on access to care for patients, it is far from clear that jury awards are the sole driving force as the President suggests.

In 2003, the Government Accountability Office studied States with and without caps on non-economic damages and found that the States with caps had lower premium increases than those without caps. However, GAO did not have enough data to show a direct link between malpractice award caps and premiums.

Similarly, the Congressional Budget Office has found that there are potential savings for malpractice premiums by limiting the amount of malpractice awards, but they are skeptical that a cap would provide relief for health care costs in general.

Malpractice costs were $24 billion in 2002, less than 2 percent of total national health care spending of $1.4 trillion, according to CBO. Reducing malpractice awards by 30 percent would only lower health care costs by approximately 0.5 percent, or about $7 billion. Granted, any lowering of health care costs would be an encouraging sign.

CBO also finds that limiting physicians' malpractice liability would not have much impact on "defensive medicine," such as providing unnecessary tests or procedures to avoid a lawsuit because physicians do so more often out of concern for patients or to generate additional income than because they fear liability.

Dr. McClellan, I know you have studied the issue of defensive medicine and malpractice, so I will be particularly interested in your opinions about the amount of health cost savings caps on noneconomic damages would produce. I believe, however, that there are some other reasons for the latest increases in medical malpractice insurance premiums that would not be addressed by the kinds of reforms the President is advocating. The GAO, for example, points to slower growth in insurance company investment income and reduced competition in the liability insurance market as other potential drivers behind rising malpractice premiums.

We also should not lose sight of the fact that this issue must be considered in the context of medical errors and the quality of patient care, which are inextricably linked to physician accountability. A study by the Institute of Medicine reported in 2000 that between 44,000 and 98,000 people die every year because of preventable medical errors. These statistics point to a need to link any discussion of tort reform to the issues of medical errors, public safety and physician accountability.

In the last Congress, the Republican leadership sent narrow medical liability legislation for OB/GYNs directly to the floor, thereby sidestepping serious committee deliberation and inquiry into the nature of and possible solutions for rising insurance premiums. While it is hard to see how the President's proposal for medical liability reform will make more than a dent in spiraling health care costs, this is an important issue that lawmakers must be allowed to investigate thoroughly.

Again, your presence here today, Dr. McClellan, as the Chairman said, is an important step in this inquiry. I appreciate your willingness to testify.

I hope you will also be open to questions regarding your oversight of CMS, which raises questions now and again. I have a number of questions regarding the $500 billion of Federal spending that you administer at CMS that undoubtedly has a bigger impact on physician behavior and overall health spending than medical malpractice costs.

I look forward to your testimony.

Thank you, Mr. Chairman.

[The prepared statement of Senator Reed appears in the Submissions for the Record on page 35.]

Representative Saxton. Dr. McClellan, welcome once again. I understand that your statement may take more than 5 minutes. That is fine. We have all morning. We are anxious to get started. You may begin, sir. The floor is yours.

STATEMENT OF MARK McCLELLAN, M.D., PH.D., ADMINISTRATOR, CENTERS FOR MEDICARE AND MEDICAID SERVICES

Dr. McClellan. Mr. Chairman, thank you for this opportunity.

Mr. Chairman, Senator Reed, Representative Hinchey, distinguished Members of the Committee, thank you for inviting me here today to discuss medical liability reform and, Senator Reed, congratulations, and I hope this isn't part of your honeymoon.

As President Bush and many in Congress and across the country recognize, our current liability system does not serve the needs of patients and needs reform. It is not simply an issue of reducing health care costs by lowering the costs of medical liability. More importantly, it is about improving patient safety and quality of care.

The Medicare and Medicaid programs are not immune from the costs created by our liability system. The Congressional Budget Office has estimated that if legislation the House has considered, and that you just mentioned, Senator Reed, were signed into law, it would result in savings to the Federal Government alone of more than $11 billion for the 2004 to 2013 period.

But this figure only considers premium reductions. It doesn't take into account the far greater savings possible as a result of reducing defensive medicine. Peer-reviewed research that I conducted with Professor Dan Kessler at Stanford University found that capping non-economic damages and revising joint and several liability rules could reduce the practice of defensive medicine so that overall hospital expenditures would drop by between 5 and 9 percent.

During fiscal year 2004, we spent more than $133 billion on hospital care in our fee-for-service Medicare program, and so that would translate to annual savings of between $6 and $11 billion. Other peer-reviewed studies have reinforced the importance of liability pressures driving broader cost increases in our health care system.

Right now, Medicare faces a real challenge with physician payments. Spending on physician services during 2004 rose by approximately 15 percent from the previous year. As we work on solutions to the physician payment problem, we can no longer afford to pass by opportunities where there is overwhelming evidence of billions of dollars in cost savings without compromising patient health.

For example, a significant driver of the past year's increase is the fact that more patients are receiving more complex and more frequent diagnostic imaging services. This is exactly the kind of medical practice that is aggravated by liability concerns.

Doctors understandably worry about being sued for bad outcomes rather than bad care, since that is mainly what happens in our current system. Doctors worry about being sued even when they follow state-of-the-art medical practice because that is what happens.

In fact, physicians get a double whammy. These liability pressures drive up costs without increasing quality, and because of the way our physician payment systems work in Medicare, when that happens, physicians get hit with reductions in payments on top of it. That can worsen the problem of access. We just can't afford to do this anymore.

The problem is seriously aggravated by the disturbing recent trends in liability settlements and awards. Mr. Chairman, you put up some of the figures showing up through 2003, which were very concerning, but on top of that, the Physician Insurance Association of America, a main insurer of physicians for liability costs, has recently noted that the average jury award increased by 46 percent between 2003 and 2004, to over $439,000, and that includes an increase in the very large awards that you mentioned. So on top of the big increases in settlements and awards in the preceding years, I fear the quality and cost problems caused by our liability system will continue to worsen.

With the new Medicare law and our proposals for Medicaid reform, we are taking many steps to support prevention-oriented care and promote better quality and safety, but it is hard to do that in an environment where legitimate worries about liability stand in the way of quality and safety improvement. That is the main reason we need liability reform through such proven measures as caps on non-economic damages.

Liability reform will improve health care quality and access and costs, leading to better health for Americans. In saying that our liability system needs reform now, I want to be very clear that I fully support the goals of liability law. These are the right goals. Patients who are injured deserve to be compensated when they are treated negligently, and we need to provide strong measures to assure that physicians and other health professionals provide high-quality care and face consequences when they are negligent. But the fact is our liability system is failing miserably at both goals.

For example, one of the most definitive studies, the Harvard Medical Practice Study, reported that, on average, it takes more than 5 years for an insurer to pay a malpractice claim after the date of the incident, and when an injured patient does finally successfully settle or win the case, the patient doesn't get most of the money.

Even worse, only a tiny fraction of those who are injured due to negligent care get even this delayed and incomplete compensation, as you noted, Mr. Chairman. So in the system we have now, most of the money that is finally awarded goes to lawyers and to patients who were not injured negligently. These are the features of a long, slow and costly lottery.

The liability system is not achieving its goals. Because doctors know they can and will be sued even when, in fact, mostly when they don't do anything wrong, it is no surprise that the result is higher health care costs and quality and access problems. The defensive medicine resulting from our liability system includes the costs and risks of unnecessary procedures, and it includes problems in access to care. In emergency care, in obstetrics, in neurosurgery and in other specialties in many areas of the country, as your chart showed, the result of high liability premiums and frustration over lawsuits is simply less access to physicians. And even if you can get access to care, it means higher costs.

Our legal system simply does not serve the needs of patients and it does not encourage physicians to practice science-based, quality medicine. The evidence is clear that Congress could reduce health care costs and improve quality by passing legislation that puts in place reasonable caps on non-economic damages and revises the joint and several liability rules that encourage lawyers to collect several times over for the same damages. Such reforms would still allow patients to get very large recoveries for their injuries, including full compensation even for services like child care that do not come with a paying job.

There are other steps that can be taken, as well, that would also help our liability system do what it is failing to do today, without adding unnecessary costs or compromising quality of care like the current system does. For example, in late 2004, the Department of Health and Human Services announced a voluntary early offers program.

Under this program when someone files a claim against the department, for example, for care in a community health center or through the Indian Health Service, HHS will evaluate the claim and then send that person a notice telling them about the option of using an early offer. Then both sides have 90 days to submit a confidential settlement offer to an independent third party. If the offers match or they overlap, the case is settled and HHS immediately pays the amount requested with much more of the money going much faster to the injured patient. If there is no match, the case can proceed as usual.

The goal of this program is to do what our liability system is failing to do, provide prompt and predictable settlements for injured patients without the delays and the uncertainty of trying to go to court. And these patients will not have to turn over a large part of their settlement to their lawyers. We need to support more steps like this.

Some time ago, Johns Hopkins Hospital began requiring non-emergency patients who came to them for elective procedures to sign an agreement to take any malpractice claims to mediation prior to going to court. In 2003, 24 cases went to mediation and 21 of them were resolved promptly. As a result, the experience for Hopkins Hospital in 2003 claims decreased in expense by almost 30 percent.

Mediation is typically much faster than a court case and involves far lower attorneys' fees. In short, patients who are injured get compensated at a higher level and in a shorter amount of time. Costs are lower and more predictable, improving the delivery of care.

We are looking at ways to encourage such steps toward better compensation and lower costs to the liability system in the Medicare program. For the sake of our patients and for quality of care, we can't afford to pass up these opportunities anymore.

Another promising idea is the establishment of special health boards or courts devoted to hearing cases involving claims of medical malpractice. These specialized courts would employ specially trained judges with health care expertise and background and would deal only with liability cases. Judges could be selected through a non-partisan process. Their expertise and impartiality would provide the predictability, the timeliness and the fair compensation that simply don't exist in our current system.

Besides looking at opportunities to provide a better compensation system for injured patients, we are also taking many steps at CMS to help patients actually get better care. This includes new systems for reporting information on the quality and safety of care in hospitals, in nursing homes, in home health agencies and, soon, in ambulatory care as well. It includes quality improvement initiatives and more coordinated work with State oversight agencies. These are effective ways to increase provider accountability.

I am also pleased about the bipartisan congressional interest in patient safety legislation that includes a mechanism for allowing anonymous reporting of errors and risky situations, and anonymous systems to help prevent those errors in the future. It protects these badly needed data from discovery. We don't have as much of this preventive information as we should because health professionals rightly fear that it would be used not to improve quality, but as the target of a fishing expedition for lawyers. The same concerns are slowing the adoption of electronic health information systems that can improve quality and safety. As the Institute of Medicine has noted, if we don't take these steps, we will keep missing opportunities to improve patient safety and quality.

Mr. Chairman, we are increasingly using performance standards in our health care system. We need to subject our liability system to this same kind of performance review. Its very low levels of performance in terms of compensating injured patients and encouraging quality care mean that it is blocking progress toward better care.

The current medical liability system is not meeting the needs of patients and it is costing those patients and the Federal Government and other payers billions of dollars because it causes unnecessary care and problems in access to care, and it is providing no reliable compensation to patients who are injured. We know how to do a lot better and we are looking forward to working with you toward liability reforms that improve quality and access to care and reduce health care costs.

I would be pleased to take any questions that you all may have.

[The prepared statement of Dr. McClellan appears in the Submissions for the Record on page 36.]

Representative Saxton. Dr. McClellan, thank you very much for an excellent statement. Let me begin by referring to something that you alluded to and that I mentioned in my opening statement.

It is quite surprising to me to find that a large majority, according to some studies, of doctors who have been subject to lawsuits—that something in the neighborhood of 80 percent of the medical liability claims don't involve negligent injuries. This has been something that I have found hard to understand. In fact, as I pointed out in my opening statement, one study found that more than half of medical liability claims don't involve any injury at all.

Can you talk a little bit about this and explain how this can be and what kind of a problem? It is obviously a big problem.

Dr. McClellan. Mr. Chairman, your figures are right. They are drawn from studies like that Harvard Medical Practice Study that took a systematic look at the cases that were coming to court. They reviewed all of the cases over a certain time period in some specific States or a large sample of cases, including cases in New York, and they found the kind of results that you are talking about.

And other follow-up studies have yielded similar results, that very often cases are brought when there are bad outcomes, even if there was no medical negligence involved, and very often there may not even be actual harm demonstrated. It may be a claim that the patient was perhaps someday at risk of harm even when, again, the physician has followed appropriate medical practices.

The system that we have now does not screen out these kinds of cases. It doesn't encourage us to focus, most importantly, on cases where there has been true negligence and, as a result, doctors should be held accountable. If we did a better job of that, we could compensate the patients who are truly injured negligently much more effectively, and we could provide more predictability to the doctors.

They wouldn't have to worry that when they are providing care that is up to standards and doing what they think is right from the standpoint of their medical expertise, they will be able to practice appropriately. They won't be hauled into court for it.

Representative Saxton. How did these studies arrive at the conclusion that all of these cases did not involve any negligent behavior?

Dr. McClellan. They involved a kind of medical review that ought to be a more systematic part of our approach to medical liability and medical negligence. They had independent expert reviewers, multiple reviewers, look at all of these cases, look at all the documentation and reach conclusions about whether appropriate medical practice was followed or not and whether the alleged injury was, in fact, from a medical standpoint, related to the actions of the doctor. It is that kind of expert involvement that we don't have in our liability system today.

Representative Saxton. Of this large percentage of cases that don't involve negligent injuries, do many of them result in awards to the claimant?

Dr. McClellan. Yes. Most of the awards that do occur are for cases where there was no negligence by the physicians. A lot of these cases end up being dropped or end up being settled for little or no money; but many of them do end up in large settlements, and even in the cases that don't end up giving money to the plaintiff, they do end up taking a lot of time and effort on the part of the doctor and the doctor's medical staff, and they do end up with a lot of the money going to the lawyers that are involved.

Representative Saxton. On the other side of this coin, I am told it is widely recognized that only a small fraction of negligently injured patients file a claim.

How can this be so backwards?

Dr. McClellan. Well, it is a very difficult system to navigate because the costs are so high, and it takes so long, and there is so much burden. There is a burden on the doctors. There are also burdens on the patients for going through this long process. A lot of them don't bother with the effort. That is why I think that some of the steps that I outlined in my written and my oral statements are so important.

If we can take steps to take these out of the court system, that is a 5-year-long process that has a lot of burdens along the way, and have a quicker approach, like this Early Offers system that I mentioned or approaches that rely on mediation, I think more patients who are truly injured negligently could get compensated, and more of the money would actually go to them. It wouldn't go to the costs of administering this very long and complicated system. It wouldn't go so much to the lawyers involved.

Representative Saxton. So to conclude this point, I guess, there are a large number of people who receive, for lack of a better term, negligent treatment who are not compensated, and there are a large number of people who receive very adequate, non-negligent treatment who get compensated.

Dr. McClellan. And then a lot of money goes to the lawyers in the process, at least 30 to 40 percent of any settlements that occur. And then there are other administrative costs for the lawyers on the other side, the courts and so forth.

Most of the money in the system doesn't end up going to patients, and you are right that only a very small fraction of it actually goes to patients who are injured negligently.

Representative Saxton. Now, of course, I am not a doctor; but I am a human being, and if I were a doctor, it would seem to me that I would go to my practice each day with a list of things that I needed to do, and perhaps one of the most important—maybe the most important—is to protect myself from potential claims. And if I were a doctor, not being one, how would I do that?

Dr. McClellan. Well, there are steps that you could take to protect yourself from claims. I think people who have studied this issue talk about positive and negative defensive medicine.

"Negative defensive medicine" is that you just stop taking the cases. If there are high-risk procedures, cases where there is some real chance of a bad outcome, like in neurosurgery or in obstetrics or in some types of emergency care, there are many doctors who are just leaving those practices.

I have talked to physicians in different parts of the country, the Mississippi Delta, the Las Vegas area, parts of Ohio, Pennsylvania, other parts of the country where there are now real access problems, particularly for certain kinds of specialties and certain kinds of procedures from doctors just staying away from them. It is not worth the risk. They can't afford the insurance. They don't want to go through the hassle when they are practicing good care.

On the other side, so-called "positive defensive medicine" costs, or extra tests and extra procedures that might be ordered not because that is what the medical guidelines say, but just because a doctor wants to be protected in the event of a suit being brought, that is where we see maybe extra cases of imaging procedures being done.

I talked about some of the rapid growth we have seen in the past year in the Medicare program, in the use of advanced imaging procedures that are very costly, and in some cases, when a patient comes in with a headache or another problem like that, that just aren't medically warranted. So we would like doctors to come to practice every morning thinking about, "What are the things that I can do today that are going to do the most for my patients at the lowest cost?" This system creates some very different kinds of pressures on how they make their decisions.

Representative Saxton. Your answer reminded me of an incident that occurred in New Jersey.

We have neurological physicians, of course, in New Jersey. At one time we had around 90. Now, I understand we have less than 60. One of the hospitals that lost their neurological surgeon had a need for one. A lady was admitted to the hospital and there was no neurological surgeon to treat her. So they literally had to get a helicopter and fly her across the river to Philadelphia for treatment. It seems to me that that would create a situation where people don't actually have access to proper care.

Dr. McClellan. It is.

On the one hand, it is higher cost because she had to get all that extra transportation. At the same time, it is worse quality of care. Many neurologic procedures are urgent. The transportation time, the disruptions that can occur in moving a patient can compromise quality of care. And so from both a quality and a cost standpoint, it is a real problem.

Representative Saxton. On the positive side, the things that you referred to as positive steps that can be taken, I suspect that very thorough examination and testing would be a way to protect myself if I were a doctor.

Dr. McClellan. That is right. And very thorough examination and testing is appropriate in many medical cases. We want doctors doing a thorough job of working up a patient appropriately, according to the latest medical science. But their decisions ought to be determined by the medical science, not the latest court verdicts where doctors are being sued successfully. So often when there hasn't been any actual medical negligence, when they are being sued unsuccessfully in a lot of cases where there is no negligence—but they still have to be dragged into court, it still takes a lot of time and effort, it still adds to their liability cost—you end up with different kinds of pressures on the way the doctors are practicing. And that is what we would really like to avoid.

Representative Saxton. It seems to me that one of the downsides of doing too many tests would have to do with expense. That goes without saying. You do tests that are, quote, "unnecessary" to protect oneself, the doctor. It is going to cost more.

Any other downsides?

Dr. McClellan. You can get into a vicious cycle. Very often when these imaging procedures are done, there may be an anomaly on the test. No test is perfect. No test is right 100 percent of the time.

If you are doing a diagnostic test on a patient that has got a very low likelihood of actually having a real problem and you see something anomalous, probably in many cases it is just going to be the fact that a test isn't perfect. But if you see that, if you have done the test in part because of liability pressures, you are going to have to do something else about it. So you may end up in a situation where you are going just from ordering an MRI to then having to go on to further workup of a patient, a biopsy procedure, other types of services that carry with them their own risks and potential for harm and additional costs.

Representative Saxton. A large percentage of the American population pays for medical care through Medicaid and Medicare. It seems to me that since older folks, in terms of Medicare, receive a very large percentage of medical treatment in this country, for obvious reasons, that there would be a particular concern with regard to the implications for Medicare and Medicaid.

Can you speak to that subject? What does it do to the system that you oversee?

Dr. McClellan. When you take account of these defensive medical costs, it means higher costs in a couple of ways. One is the higher costs associated with the extra procedures, the extra tests and so forth. Another is the higher costs associated with complications of problems of access to care. If patients can't get access to the neurosurgical services they need, or the emergency services or other problems, that can lead to higher costs as well. It certainly leads to quality problems.

Some of the studies that I have been involved with, these peer-reviewed studies published in academic journals, suggest that we could have an impact on Medicare costs of 5 percent or more, at least for hospital costs, by addressing these defensive medicine problems, by reforming our liability system.

Even if you are only looking at the direct costs of the higher liability premiums and the costs of the liability system itself, again money that is mainly not going to care for patients and not going to compensate patients who are injured negligently, even there you can save billions of dollars in program reforms as that CBO study that Senator Reed mentioned documented. There are real opportunities for lowering costs, and that is something that we need to be paying a lot of attention to right now when we are struggling to find ways to pay our physicians appropriately, and when we are trying to take steps to make our program as sustainable as possible.

Representative Saxton. Tell us about the effect on the Medicare trust fund.

Dr. McClellan. The savings that these reforms would engender, the billions of dollars in savings, according to CBO estimates, the even larger savings that could result from really doing something about defensive medicine, would assist the trust funds. That would reduce the pressure that the trust funds are facing.

I won't say this is the only step that we need to take to make sure Medicare is sustainable. We also need to bring our benefits up to date and take other steps that promote higher-quality care as I talked about.

But we really want to create an environment that encourages high-quality medical practice and that avoids unnecessary costs, and the liability system that we have today is standing right in the way of that goal.

Representative Saxton. One of the answers to this problem appears to be something that is referred to as "caps on non-economic damages." These caps have been touted as an important element of effective medical liability reform, and I referred to the one chart.

Maybe we could put that chart back up again, the one that is right there in the front. That is good.

The national average for premium growth since 1976 up until 2003 is demonstrated here by this chart as a relatively flat line in the case of California, which enacted caps in 1975 and a very steep inclining rate of growth for the national average.

I am told that Kenneth Thorpe of Emory University recently—and incidentally a former Clinton Administration health official—came to the conclusion that premiums in States with a cap on awards were significantly lower, as is depicted by this chart, than States without caps.

Would you discuss this?

Dr. McClellan. It is not just Dr. Thorpe's conclusion. It is also the conclusion of studies that have been done by the policy and evaluation office in the Department of Health and Human Services. It is the result of studies that we have done and that have been published in peer-reviewed academic journals before I came to work in Government. It has been the result of other studies by other distinguished economists and health policy researchers.

From these studies, together they show that these kinds of caps on non-economic lead to changes in physician behavior because the physicians feel less pressured to deal with liability and more focused on providing care for their patients. They lead to lower costs of defensive medicine, as we have already talked about a little bit. They lead to lower liability premiums because they reduce the costs of our liability system. And they lead to greater access to care.

A recent study by the Agency for Health Care Research and Quality showed that in States that have implemented these liability reforms, they have a significantly larger number of physicians in practice. So you have less situations like the one that you described in New Jersey where a patient can't get access to the care they need.

Representative Saxton. If caps were successful in bringing about these changes in medical care and the performance and activities of physicians, would it also be fair to say that it would have the effect of reducing the costs of the actual premiums charged to doctors?

Dr. McClellan. It would have a direct effect on reducing the premiums; that is correct.

The beneficiaries in the Medicare program pay a quarter of the costs for Medicare Part B, and that is the cost of physician services and all the other outpatient services, including all those imaging procedures and lab tests and so forth. So it would have a direct effect on premiums.

Representative Saxton. Would it have an effect on the cost to the consumer?

Dr. McClellan. It would also have an effect on the cost to consumers. Not just because of lower premiums, but because if they are undergoing fewer tests, if they are getting medical care that is practiced more efficiently where they can get the relief they need for their health problems at a lower cost—that is, lower copays, as well, and lower out-of-pocket payments for that reason, too.

Representative Saxton. In your opening statement you mentioned—along with caps for medical liability tort reform involving caps on non-economic damages, you also mentioned mediation.

Dr. McClellan. Yes.

Representative Saxton. Would you explain the effect of how you see mediation working?

Dr. McClellan. Mediation is just a better environment for getting to resolution of issues in a way that reflects the medical science. Mediation is led by an independent expert, someone who knows the field of medicine and who is not on one side or the other, who can work to try to bring the different sides together.

I mentioned the Johns Hopkins Hospital case where now this is mandatory for patients who are coming in for elective non-urgent procedures. They have time to think about whether they want to get care this way, and mostly, generally, they decide that they want to.

The cases—if there is a problem of a bad outcome or other dispute, go to mediation instead of going straight to a court in that long, 5-year-or-longer, lottery to get to resolution. The mediation can take place in a matter of a few months because there is less court time and less lawyer time involved.

The money involved in the mediation settlement goes to the patient who is injured, and because you have got an independent expert involved in getting to a conclusion, you are more likely to reflect the actual medical facts and have a decision that is predictable based on what medical science says it should be.

Representative Saxton. I apologize to Senator Reed. I have one final question and then we will go to Senator Reed.

We know that the medical liability crisis has not hit all specialties in the same way. Obstetricians, orthopedic surgeons, neurosurgeons and radiologists have been hit particularly hard. It would seem that the higher premiums charged to these specialties would have an impact on which areas of the medical profession students choose to enter. So the question is fairly obvious.

Looking down the road, do we see any problem in finding specialists in certain areas that are especially hit negatively by this medical malpractice situation?

Dr. McClellan. It is certainly a concern. When I talk to my colleagues who are still in academic medical practice, they note that this is having an impact on student decisions. That will have consequences down the road. But I think even more worrisome is, it is having some consequences now.

I have talked about some of the evidence on different levels of access to physicians in conjunction with whether or not a State has reformed its liability system; and as you put up on your chart earlier, there are areas of the country where physicians are leaving practice, particularly in these specialties, where they are not taking the more complex cases in these specialties right now.

So this isn't a problem that is just down the road, that will be aggravated by the decisions that medical students are making today about specialties to avoid because of liability concerns; it is a problem right now in many areas of the country.

Representative Saxton. Thank you very much.

Senator Reed.

Senator Reed. Well, thank you, Mr. Chairman. I wonder if we could have a second round, and I can limit my questions and allow my colleagues to ask their questions without an extended period.

Thank you very much, Dr. McClellan, for your testimony and for your work. In fact, back in 1996, you and Dr. Kessler did a path-breaking study of the effects of defensive medicine. You estimated the costs to be somewhere between 5 and 9 percent. Others have looked at the same issue, CBO for one, and have not found as great an impact.

Do you have any insights as to why CBO would find a much less——

Dr. McClellan. Senator Reed, I know you pay a lot of attention to these economic issues, and I appreciate the question. We had a little bit of discussion of this in my written testimony. When CBO looked at the same conditions we did, they found similar results.

So looking just at heart disease—these are pretty well defined cases. There is an event that occurred, a patient having a heart attack or other serious heart problem, then we tracked after that. When CBO looked in the same way, they found the same kinds of effects.

But the problem with the CBO study is that it also looked at other types of cases, just sort of the overall population of patients; and that is a very heterogeneous set of patients, some of which have certain diseases, others have other diseases. And there are a lot of things that influence costs of care in these patients and their outcomes of care. And so, in economic terms, that means this is a noisier or less precise estimation situation.

They also had only a proportion of the cases, not the whole larger sample that we looked at. And so it is probably not surprising that they didn't get to as statistically significant results.

The other thing is that in the cases that we were looking at, these were cases where people were already getting care. They had come into the hospital with a very serious medical problem.

In the cases that CBO looked at, they would also pick up cases where people may not get treatment. Remember, there are two kinds of defensive medicine. There is defensive medicine that leads to higher costs and perhaps a worse outcome, and there is also defensive medicine where the doctors just don't take the cases, that leads to less access to care. They probably were mixing up some of both. There may well be some, quote-unquote, savings from doctors not seeing patients. But I am not sure that is a good thing.

The bottom line, though, is that CBO concluded, as you mentioned earlier, that reforming the liability system would save Medicare billions of dollars. We can argue about what the magnitude of those savings should be, but there is no question, all these studies say "significant savings," and that is something that I think is really important to take advantage of.

Senator Reed. But your study was more precisely related to those heart procedures?

Dr. McClellan. Those heart conditions, right.

Senator Reed. That is where you would see that, based on your——

Dr. McClellan. Potentially in others. I think there have been some other studies done of care for patients with other particular conditions, obstetrical conditions, deliveries, where you see similar kinds of effects. More use of Cesarean sections, for example, in States that haven't reformed their liability systems.

When you look at particular types of illnesses where we can really define the cases clearly, there is not this big heterogeneity problem. You tend to see effects.

Senator Reed. One of the other measures of whether this works or not is what the actors in the economic system do. Interestingly enough, in Texas, which adopted caps on non-economic damages, GE Medical Protective, a large insurer, made a regulatory filing where they estimated that capping non-economic damages will show loss savings of 1 percent. Again, 1 percent of a big number is real money, but they requested a premium increase of 19 percent 1 year after Texas capped their non-economic damages.

One of the assumptions implicit in most of the discussion we had this morning is that if you cap non-economic damages, you will reduce premiums for malpractice insurance. Here is a situation where they are asking—and they are economic actors looking at their costs—for a significant increase and they estimate that there is a saving from the cap, but relatively small.

What is going on down there?

Dr. McClellan. Well, I think they are looking at the so-called "direct liability costs" or this impact on liability premiums, and there are other savings that would come from the impacts on defensive medicine. That is not something that the liability insurer is actually going to see. That is something that our health care system is going to see as a result of differences in medical practice.

But as you have said, a percentage point reduction in medical spending, that is still real money, and in a big health care system, that is still billions of dollars.

They also are facing price increases in Texas for other reasons. That Texas liability reform didn't do everything that I think the kinds of damage caps that we have talked about would do. But just to put this in perspective, if you look at the 75-year actuarial deficit for the Hospital Insurance trust fund, that is, the Medicare Part A trust fund that people are really concerned about because it is scheduled to become insolvent in 2020, we could get rid of two-thirds of the 75-year deficit by reducing the rate of growth in medical spending by 1 percentage point.

So if we change the way medicine is practiced, even if it is incremental, it really adds up to savings over time.

Senator Reed. Let me focus on the point that there is an implicit assumption that if you cap medical non-economic awards, you will reduce medical premiums; and here you have a company who is saying, "You've done that. Terrific. Now give us a 19 percent increase."

I would also suggest, as many others did, that the California experience was shaped not just by the 1985 law capping damages, but by the 1988 law that actually imposed limits on the increasing size of malpractice premiums.

Dr. McClellan. As you saw from the chart, the slowdown in growth started before 1988, and it has continued well after.

Senator Reed. But my point with respect to the premiums that physicians are paying is that the result was not simply the adoption of caps on non-economic damages, but also limits on malpractice premiums.

Would you support, in conjunction with a proposal for tort reform or insurance reform, putting caps on insurance premiums?

Dr. McClellan. I certainly want to see how such a proposal would actually work. If you put caps on premiums, but don't change the liability system, for example, you will end up with insurers not being able to cover the rapidly rising costs of claims that we are seeing.

If you look at the claims growth in recent years, including that 40 percent increase that I mentioned between 2003 and 2004, you are going to end up without liability insurance and then you are really going to end up with doctors out of practice.

Senator Reed. But the other side of the equation is, if you cap non-economic damages, but don't put any limits on insurance premiums, you could have the situation as there seems to be in Texas with GE Medical where they get the benefit of the law and they still ask for a 19 percent increase. That, I think, would be unfortunate because, again, a lot of this debate is being driven by the implicit and sometimes explicit assumption that if you cap damages, you lower premiums to physicians and hospitals and other health care providers, and they go on their merry way. Which raises the other issue behind why premiums are going up, why medical costs are going up, and that is the technology, allowing increased procedures.

It is interesting. You mentioned the diagnostic imaging procedures. I had my radiologists from Rhode Island in. Their major comment—I won't say "complaint" because they never complain—their comment was internists, general practitioners are now getting very good, digitized equipment to do radiological procedures. It is not the old bulky kind that required a little more practice and training. It is secondhand equipment, though it is still adequate; and because they are under acute pressure in their offices to generate income, they are doing tests which before they might not do. Because it is so easy to do it, they can step in the next room and now give you a little scan with their radiological equipment.

How much of these costs and these increased procedures are being generated by access to technology and the pressure, because of the way we pay people through Medicare, to generate these procedures to get more income?

Dr. McClellan. Senator Reed, I think you are right that the way that we pay in Medicare also doesn't necessarily focus on getting the best-quality care at the lowest cost.

We are having some discussions right now with the radiologists, with other medical groups, about how we can get to a better system, where our payment rules are focusing more on supporting doctors, delivering high-quality care at a low cost.

I would be delighted to continue to work with you on that issue. But I think the fact remains that you are right, that it is easy now for physicians to obtain this imaging equipment and to bill for it. But the liability pressures on top of that are just going to encourage that even more. So I think we should be looking at better ways to formulate Medicare payments, to support and reward doctors that are really trying to do the right thing.

But we can also do that by reforming the liability system. If we do both together, we are going to have a much better effect.

Senator Reed. Again, I think what your comments suggest and what my instincts are is, this is a multifaceted problem requiring multifaceted approaches. But we seem to hear the Administration use one approach, which is basically, if we just rein in those junk lawsuits, everything is fine, when in fact I think you would concede, we have a complicated medical delivery system that has all sorts of different incentives and disincentives.

Dr. McClellan. That is true, but I also think if we rein in the lawsuits, we will get higher-quality care, better access and lower cost.

There are other things that we should be doing to achieve that goal as well. I hope we can work together on them, too.

Senator Reed. Well, Mr. Chairman, again I think this is very productive. I appreciate Dr. McClellan's presence. But I would—in lieu of a second round, let me just stop and let my colleagues go.

Representative Saxton. Mr. Hinchey.

Representative Hinchey. Good morning, Dr. McClellan, thank you very much for your testimony.

The licensing of professionals, including medical professionals and specialties in medicine, and the regulation of those professions is an activity that is carried out by the various States. And various States, as we have seen in one of the charts, have taken various steps over the years to deal with the problem of medical malpractice, including the regulation of lawsuits, as well as other steps.

Why is this a Federal issue? Why should the Federal Government be involved in trying to limit people's access to the courts?

Dr. McClellan. Two reasons. One is that the Federal Government is involved in providing access to medical care for these individuals. In our Medicare programs and our Medicaid programs, we are the primary insurer. And how we provide this care, how we provide the support for medical care, makes a big difference.

So I care a lot about the quality of care that our beneficiaries are receiving. And I also care a lot about the cost of these programs. I want to make them as sustainable as possible so that Medicare beneficiaries and Medicaid beneficiaries, who really need our help, can get the greatest help possible, can get the best access to up-to-date treatments that are really making a difference in their lives.

When I look around the country, in these States that haven't reformed their liability systems, seeing a lot of the money going into areas that are unnecessary procedures and that are problems in access to care, I really think we can do better.

Representative Hinchey. I think we can always do better in every field. But I still wonder why the Federal Government should be putting itself into this situation when it is, traditionally, for all the time in our history, that we have left this particular situation to the States to deal with, to regulate, and they have done so in various ways.

So I am not convinced that just because we have Medicare, we should be stepping in to try to limit people's access to the courts.

But I do agree with you that we ought to be doing everything that we can to try to reduce the cost of our health care services.

I am wondering if you could tell me how much money we would save if, say for Medicare particularly, if you were allowed to negotiate with the pharmaceutical companies for the cost of prescription drugs.

Dr. McClellan. Well, that is a very good question, one that there has been a lot of interest from Congress and the public in. For that reason, I have been asking my actuaries, our independent actuaries that do these forecasts of Medicare costs, about what the impact would be. And I can send you a copy of the letter that my chief actuary, Rick Foster, sent to me on this very topic back in February.

What he concluded was that negotiation by the Federal Government, on top of, or instead of, all of the negotiation that is going on right now as we implement the Medicare drug law to get the lowest possible prices to seniors—that additional negotiation would not lead to significantly lower costs and could potentially cause problems in access to care.

So the reason for that conclusion is that people have looked at what happens when the Government does step in and regulate drug prices. In Medicare, what we saw before the Medicare law was passed was prices that were higher, much higher, than can be obtained in a competitive system for the drugs that Medicare covers now under Part B.

They have looked at problems that could arise in access to care. The way that the Government could potentially negotiate is by saying, people won't get these drugs unless you give us some kind of lower price. And the result would be problems in access to the drugs.

I think it is very important, as we implement the Medicare law, that people have access to the medicines that they need, that they can get the drugs that best meet their needs. So for those kinds of reasons, our independent actuaries concluded that this wouldn't lead to more savings.

The independent analysts at CBO have reached a similar conclusion as well.

Representative Hinchey. Well, I would like very much to see that letter.

Dr. McClellan. I will send it right along.

[The information referred to can be found in the Submissions for the Record on page 44.]

Representative Hinchey. Sometimes independent actuaries turn out to be not quite so independent as you would like them to be.

Dr. McClellan. I think ours have a pretty good tradition of speaking what they think is right.

Representative Hinchey. I would like to see the letter to see what the conclusions were that they drew. And particularly in light of the fact that in every situation, in every country where you have a system of health care, national health care, and the price of pharmaceuticals are negotiated by that organization, the prices of drugs are very, very much lower than they are here, every single country.

Dr. McClellan. Well, it is true for some new drugs. I don't think it is true across the board. And it is certainly not true for the generic drugs that make up a majority of the medicines that people use in this country.

When you put price regulations on generics, you end up with higher prices, so what we see in these other countries that you are mentioning is they may have some lower costs on the new drugs that they have access to, but they do not have access to as many as we do.

But they have got higher drug costs and less access to generics, and the result is, they are spending money in a way that does not lead to the best value for their citizens.

Representative Hinchey. That is not true in the case of Canada, for example. And the Canadians have access to every single drug that we have access to.

Dr. McClellan. We will give you the specifics on that too. But there are a number of drugs that are available in the United States that haven't been available or are available with a significant delay in Canada, and you have to go through a Government system for access to many drugs, including proton pump inhibitors, AIDS drugs.

There are some drugs that are non-preferred or off formulary in Canada. There is a study. We will get all of the specifics; I don't have them all at the tip of my tongue. But there is a study done by, again, the Assistant Secretary for Planning and Evaluation that documented all of these back in 2002.

But there are AIDS treatments that were available only after substantial delay, compared to the United States, and many of the drugs that are available in Canada you have to go through Government processes in order to get. And the generic drugs in Canada do average about 40 to 50 percent higher in price than the drugs here. And generics account for most prescriptions in the United States.

Representative Hinchey. Well, I have never heard that before. That is an interesting point.

Dr. McClellan. We would like to follow up with you.

[The information referred to can be found in the Submissions for the Record on page 46.]

Representative Hinchey. When you look at the overall cost of prescription drugs, not generics specifically, but generics included in the overall cost of prescription drugs, the cost of those drugs is substantially lower. That comes about as a result of the fact that the agency in charge of the health care system there, such as Medicare, has the authority to negotiate with the pharmaceutical companies, and therefore they are able to bring down the cost of those drugs specifically.

So you have looked, outside of this letter from the actuaries, at the benefits that might accrue, the financial benefits, if you were able to negotiate?

Dr. McClellan. In the process of passing the Medicare law, there were a lot of discussions about this in Congress, as you know. Subsequently, as we have implemented the law, we have asked repeatedly, What is the best way to achieve two goals? One, we want to get prices down for drugs as much as possible for our seniors; and two, we want to make sure that seniors have access to up-to-date medicines.

What we have seen too often in Medicare, where we have relied on Government regulation and statutes only, rather than giving people access to choices about how they get their coverage, is, the benefits fall way behind. We have fallen way behind in prevention, we have fallen way behind on assistance for people with chronic illnesses and preventing complications. We have fallen way behind on prescription drugs.

So the steps that we are taking, as reflected in that actuarial letter, are the ones that are going to get us the best access to medicines and the best prices on those medicines at the same time. We need to achieve both goals.

Representative Hinchey. Well, I look forward to reading that letter. When do you think you can get it to me?

Dr. McClellan. Today.

Representative Hinchey. There is another aspect to this, too, of course. And the availability of drugs does not mean that they are available to everyone. There are many people who cannot afford drugs that become available. And so the consequence is that they are not able to take them; it is not likely that you are going to have access to those drugs.

There is just one other thing that I would like to ask in this particular round, if I may, and that is that many of the studies that I have seen that have been conducted by States indicate that a small portion of the medical profession is responsible for most of the malpractice cases and actions. And some of those doctors, if they are convicted of medical malpractice in one State, move to another State.

Do you think it would be an idea that we might pursue to have someone form a Federal oversight of physicians who are guilty of malpractice and who seek to escape that by moving to other States?

Dr. McClellan. I think having better information available on the quality of providers, including physicians, is really important. And we are taking a lot of steps to make that happen right now. We started reporting information, for example, on the quality of care on just about every hospital in the country. We started that a month ago.

We are going to expand that. We are going to make this work for ambulatory care, as well.

So I think steps in the direction of providing better information so we can identify potentially problematic providers is very important. But in terms of the cases that are actually brought, while only a relatively small share of doctors are sued frequently, in the specialties that we have talked about before, in OB, neurosurgery, most doctors have been sued at least once, if not more often.

And that gets back to this lottery problem that I talked about. Sure it would be nice to find a system, better ideas for targeting those really problematic physicians that are a small part of the total.

But most doctors are being sued. Our current system is not doing a good job of targeting in on truly bad physicians.

Representative Hinchey. True.

Representative Saxton. If I may, if we can go to Mr. Cummings, inasmuch as we are going to have a vote.

Representative Cummings. Thank you very much, Mr. Chairman.

Doctor, I want to pick up where you just left off. You say that most physicians are sued. And I am just wondering, there have been a number of proposals that there be more of a screening process early on to eliminate the so-called frivolous cases. Do you think that would help?

Dr. McClellan. I think it could help. And as I mentioned earlier and was talked about in my written testimony, right in Baltimore at Johns Hopkins Hospital, they have this automatic, or this required, process to go to mediation first for elective cases, you know, where the patient has a chance to think about it and signs a form before they get care at Hopkins, saying that they are going to mediation first.

And that works. The vast majority of complaints that are brought, get settled quickly and effectively through mediation. They never have to go to court.

Mr. Cummings. And as one who—I support Johns Hopkins, of course, I have a lot of constituents that work there. But Johns Hopkins has had its share of suits, too, sadly—I mean, that have been—I mean, with substantial awards; and in some instances, they basically just about admitted liability from the very beginning.

I can think of two right off the top of my head, and cases of death. And that is not knocking Johns Hopkins, because it is a great institution. But even in a great institution like Hopkins, things do happen.

I guess, as I sit here and I listen to my colleagues and I listen to you, I cannot help but think about something that my good friend, Senator Obama, talks about; and he talks about an empathy deficit in our country, an empathy deficit.

You have got the California law that puts a $250,000 cap on economic, non-economic loss. That was enacted, when, in 1975?

Dr. McClellan. Right.

Mr. Cummings. Do you consider this the gold standard for what the country should be doing?

Dr. McClellan. I think it is one important step the country can take to get better quality care, better access and lower cost. There are other things that we can do as well.

Mr. Cummings. Let's talk about the victim for a moment.

I do not what kind of house you live in. But if you bought a house 30 years ago for $50,000, I would hate to think that now, today, 30 years later, it is still valued at $50,000, you could just sell it for $50,000.

And I was just wondering, do you think that that figure is a little low, considering it is 30 years old, the $250,000?

Dr. McClellan. We can talk about what the figure is. When I think about these cases of damages, what I look at is the overall compensation that the victim receives. And the costs for raising a child, the cost for losses on the job, the cost for other services performed around the home, even for someone who is not working, all of those costs are fully compensated in this kind of system.

And those numbers have been going up and up and up, along with the economic costs, along with it. And if the costs of a house—those are determined by economics. The costs of wages, the costs of providing for your child, the costs of caring for your child, those have real economic implications; and those can all go up over time.

Representative Cummings. My point is, so you would expect—we can be 100 years from now and we are still at—in other words, at the time that they passed the law, they must have felt comfortable about $250,000 and what its value was at that moment. I understand they haven't changed it.

But my point still remains, I just used the house as an example that things do go up, we consider it. There is nobody sitting in this room that would accept the same salary they received 30 years ago, today; they would not do it. Nobody.

And I know that salary, given inflation and other things going up, people expect it to increase. And I am just curious, considering that, does it make sense to leave the non-economic damages cap there, considering what I just said?

Dr. McClellan. Well, again for salaries and other things like that, those go up with the costs going up in the economy. That is not subject to the cap.

Representative Cummings. You are still missing my point. My point is, do you leave it at $250,000 thirty years later.

Dr. McClellan. Again, if you are looking at a system that can lead to lower costs without causing problems with access to care, this is definitely something that can do it.

If I can say just one thing, and I have heard Senator Obama talk about the empathy deficit too, and I think the real concern here is that patients who are injured negligently just have no chance really in the court system. Only a very small fraction of them are actually able to bring cases all of the way through this very long and complicated and costly process. Those that do make it through, most of the money goes to lawyers, they don't get any compensation until years after the event has happened.

We ought to be able to do much better than that. The system is failing in compensating people who do deserve compensation for their negligent care.

Representative Cummings. Well, Mr. Chairman, I know we have got a vote. I will follow up with some written questions.

Representative Saxton. We do have a vote on a rule for consideration of the budget report. So we are going to recess for a few minutes. We will recess for about 15 minutes.

[Recess taken.]

Representative Saxton. Dr. McClellan, first of all, I apologize. Nothing I can do about it, obviously, when we have votes. But I apologize to Senator Reed, too.

I think that Senator Reed may have a couple of more questions. So let us go to Senator Reed.

Senator Reed. Thank you, Mr. Chairman.

Dr. McClellan, just a couple of follow-up questions. One is a point that Mr. Hinchey made.

One would like to think that every physician in the United States is excellently prepared, trained, unburdened by the woes of the world, et cetera, but that is not the case. In fact, you can probably posit there is a normal distribution of skills and of temperamental characteristics.

It is not surprising, then, that there is a portion on one side of the curve that seems to be involved in lots of issues of medical malpractice.

Has anyone done an estimate, since we are talking about what we can do to bring down the price of health care, that would show the savings through malpractice premiums and systemic savings by more thoroughly regulating and identifying and either retraining or redeploying these individuals?

Dr. McClellan. I haven't seen any specific savings estimates on that. I can tell you that as long as most of the lawsuits that are brought, most of the claims that are brought, are not related to negligent care, you know, there is only so much that you can do to focus in on providing better oversight for those really problematic physicians.

I think, as part of liability reform, if we were able to take a lot of these inappropriate lawsuits off the table, then we could really concentrate our efforts on those problem physicians.

Senator Reed. I do not want to be unnecessarily argumentative, but based upon observation and not analysis, most people understand in the profession, other doctors, who is competent, who is attentive. Complaints are made to medical societies. This is a mostly secret process at the local level by medical societies, and there are reasons for that, obviously.

But it seems to me that you are kind of, you know, missing the point if you are suggesting we have to reform the tort system before we can focus on what may be another cause of medical malpractice, costs, and basic quality of care. Now that gets us into a whole set of issues, local licensure versus a Federal role, et cetera; but again I think, if we do not look at that, then we are not being——

Dr. McClellan. I think that is a legitimate point. I am saying that the tort system as it is now is drawing in a lot of physicians who are practicing perfectly good, if not stellar, care into lawsuits and into all of those additional pressures and costs associated with the liability.

There is a foundation to build on now. There is now a national practitioner database that the Agency for Health Care Research and Quality maintains. And that is intended to be a repository of information on claims that may be brought in different States and so forth. And it can be used by hospitals, by other health care organizations, and by States in accreditation issues for doctors.

Senator Reed. My final point, I think it would be extremely useful in this overall debate to try to quantify what is going on here with respect to the quality issues and the capability issues of physicians. Because if there were—I do not know, but if there were equal savings in that arena, or even greater savings vis-a-vis capping damages, certainly that is something that we would want to know about.

Let me shift gears to something else under your jurisdiction, the Part D drug benefit. You are implementing it now. Many States, like my own, Rhode Island, have their own local programs. We have something called RIPAE, the Rhode Island State Pharmacy Assistance Program.

There is some confusion about benefits. There is confusion about who is qualified for what. We have more robust benefits at the State level in certain circumstances, the Federal program has other benefits.

Bottom-line question: What are you doing to try to address this issue, not just for Rhode Island, but particularly for Rhode Island?

Dr. McClellan. Senator, we are doing a lot. And I hope, if you have been talking to any Rhode Island State officials who do not feel completely plugged into CMS right now on how to make these programs continue to work and actually improve with the implementation of the drug benefit, you will get them in touch with me and our agency right away.

I just got back from a conference sponsored by the National Governors Association in Chicago, where representatives of almost every State government that have been working with us on implementing the new drug benefit, came together to take stock of where we are and what the further problems are that we need to address.

We had some excellent discussions about the materials that we have already prepared for transitioning dual-eligibles, to steps that we are taking to make sure that every State saves money under the law as intended. And I feel very good about the track that we are on.

In the case of programs that provided prescription drug assistance, like the Rhode Island program, the intent of the law is to build on that. So instead of the State having to pick up all of the costs on their own, the Federal Government is going to provide some comprehensive help for low-income beneficiaries. The State will have to pay virtually nothing, and more than $1,000 worth of help for higher-income beneficiaries, so the State can add to that.

We have guidance and work groups that are working right now to make sure that that gets implemented smoothly. So if there are any concerns there, they need to come to us. We have got processes in place.

Senator Reed. Thank you.

Representative Saxton. Thank you. Sorry to have held you up, Jack.

Dr. McClellan, a good doctor-patient relationship has always been considered to be a crucial element of a medical care program—caring doctors and trusting patients, I would characterize it.

In a recent survey of Pennsylvania doctors, they found that 75 percent of specialists agreed with the following statement, quote, “Because of concerns about malpractice, I view every patient as a potential malpractice lawsuit,” end quote.

Seventy-five percent of the doctors agreed with that statement. I am wondering, given that, what is the current nature of the doctor-patient relationship generally with specialists, and are you concerned about it?

Dr. McClellan. I am very concerned about it. That gets back to what you brought up before, Mr. Chairman, about the fact that since most of the claims and suits that are actually brought do not involve negligent care, doctors have to view this sort of system as a lottery, as just a random risk of lots of time in court, lots of opportunities for lawyers to rake their reputations over the coals unfairly; and that clearly is going to have an impact on their relationship with patients, on how they practice.

It can have an impact on how they practice medicine. It may have an impact on whether they stay in the profession.

Pennsylvania is one of the States that is in red because of some documented problems in access to care, resulting from the rising pressures of medical liability. As I said at the outset, I worry that is getting worse. We are seeing big increases—according to the Physician Insurance Association of America and other groups, big increases in the liability pressures that doctors are facing, most of it completely unrelated to negligent care. That is not a good situation when we are trying to really focus on delivering high-quality care at a low cost and focusing on fostering that doctor-patient relationship.

Representative Saxton. Do you have any information relating to—obviously, the rising cost of malpractice insurance itself is an issue to doctors, and a health care cost driver. But there is another set of activities that you have referred to today as practice of defensive medicine.

What percentage of the rise in health costs would you attribute—or do you have a way to do this—would you attribute to practice of the defensive medicine in conjunction with the actual cost of increases in medical malpractice?

Dr. McClellan. The best estimates from our peer reviewed, published studies are that that can be 5 to 9 percent of hospital costs for serious medical conditions. Our studies looked at heart disease, which is the single most prevalent type of illness in the country.

Other studies have looked at obstetrical care. They find increases as well. While the exact number may be hard to pin down, it is significant, it is much larger than the costs of the liability premiums alone.

Representative Saxton. Let me turn over to the insurer side. One of the issues that occurs, which creates a problem and a medical liability crisis, is that insurers actually withdraw from the market. Obviously, insurance companies have to make a profit or they cannot stay in business. Rising claims costs may simply make this line of insurance unprofitable.

Dr. McClellan. That is correct, and we have seen insurance companies pull out of this business. There are, in many States, maybe one option available, if that, for getting liability insurance. That is not a good recipe for getting liability insurance costs down.

If we had a more predictable liability system, where insurers could manage and anticipate the risk more effectively, we would see lower liability insurance premiums from more competition and a healthier insurance market.

But the liability insurance market is struggling in many States, and that is another aggravation, another consequence of the problems that we have with our liability system today. Insurers are there to deal with risk, But insurers like predictable risk. If you have got a lottery system where in 1 year costs can increase 40 percent for reasons that have nothing to do with things that you can easily predict, like the quality of medical practice, then it is a much tougher line of business. And we are seeing the consequences of that with insurers pulling out, and with some of the premium increases that have been mentioned.

Representative Saxton. Back to the doctors. Most malpractice claims are dismissed or dropped before ever reaching trial. And among those that do reach trial, most end in a verdict for the defense.

However, even if doctors are exonerated by trial, they still suffer significant costs in terms of legal fees, stress, time away from their practice, and out-of-pocket expenses.

Can you discuss, if you would, the impact on doctors of being sued, even if the claims are ultimately dismissed?

Dr. McClellan. There is a lot of good direct evidence on that. There have been surveys done nationally. And you can use that survey information to compare a doctor's outlook on their practice, the way that they practice in States that have implemented liability reforms to those that haven't.

What you see is, in States without reforms, the doctors feel the consequences of this pressure more. They feel like they have got to do more tests, they feel more frustrated with their practice of medicine. They actually spend more time away from their patients dealing with the consequences of the lawsuits.

All of these things add to health care costs, without improving the quality of medical care, and compromise the ability of doctors to deliver high-quality care to all of their patients.

Representative Saxton. There are—as Mr. Reed or Mr. Hinchey pointed out, there are a lot of other factors that go into what we have seen in the spike in the cost of medical care: new kinds of treatment, inflationary pressures of various kinds, labor rates, and so on.

Do you have any information that would help us understand how serious the malpractice component is in the overall costs, increasing costs of medical care?

Dr. McClellan. Well, from the previous studies, again 5 to 9 percent cost differences in hospital spending that can be saved by implementing liability reforms. That adds up over time to some big savings. As I said before, if we can bring down the rate of growth in our hospital costs by 1 percentage point, that is two-thirds of the 75-year deficit for Part A, the Hospital Insurance trust fund.

That is a huge impact on medical costs in this country. And some of these increases in costs are clearly worth it. Many new technologies bring new cures to patients, bring better quality of life. But as we spend more on some of these valuable new technologies to come along, to keep health care affordable, we have got to pay even more attention to getting rid of unnecessary costs in the system. That is why I think it is even more urgent; especially with the recent increases in liability costs that I documented in 2004, it is even more urgent to take action on liability reform.

Representative Saxton. Thank you very much, Dr. McClellan. I don't believe that I have any further questions at this point. I would just say that we have been dealing with this subject on this committee because we think it is extremely important, and we thank you for being here today and for your input.

I also suspect that the House will pass a reform measure this year. I wish I could suspect that the Senate would do the same, but we will see.

So we thank you for being here today to discuss these important matters with us. And we look forward to working with you as we go forward.

[Whereupon, at 11:50 a.m., the hearing was adjourned.]

Submissions for the Record

PREPARED STATEMENT OF REPRESENTATIVE JIM SAXTON, CHAIRMAN

It is a pleasure to welcome Dr. Mark McClellan before the Committee this morning to address medical liability reform.

Dr. McClellan brings a wealth of experience and knowledge to bear on this subject. Currently, Dr. McClellan serves as the Administrator of the Centers for Medicare and Medicaid Services, overseeing approximately one-third of health care spending in the U.S. In addition to being a board-certified physician in Internal Medicine, Dr. McClellan is also a Ph.D. economist. He has previously served as the Commissioner of the Food and Drug Administration and as a member of President Bush's Council of Economic Advisers.

There is little doubt that our nation's medical liability laws need reform. Over the past few years, premiums have skyrocketed. In just the last five years, total medical liability costs jumped 47%, to a record high of nearly $27 billion. One of the central cost drivers is rising claims costs. According to the legal research firm Jury Verdict Research, the median trial award for medical liability claims stands at an incredible $1.2 million, and a recent Department of Justice study reported that nearly two-thirds of medical liability trial awards exceed $250,000.

This rise in costs has reached the point where the quality and availability of health care suffer. Faced with premiums increasing 20%, 30%, or more per year, many doctors are cutting back on the scope and availability of their services. Nowhere is this trend more apparent than in obstetrics, where numerous OB/GYNs have decided it is just easier to drop the OB part altogether. Some doctors have elected early retirement or have relocated away from high litigation areas. Emergency rooms and trauma centers have also been hurt by the current crisis. The threat of lawsuits has made the practice of defensive medicine commonplace, and as a result, patients are subjected to more tests and procedures than may be warranted by clinical factors alone.

Despite the rise in costs, the system is not better at compensating the negligently injured. The typical time that elapses between the date of injury and a jury verdict is close to 5 years. Moreover, it is widely recognized that only a small fraction of negligently-injured patients even file a claim. At the same time, a large majority—around 80%—of medical liability claims do not even involve negligent injuries. One study even found that more than half of all medical liability claims do not involve an injury at all.

The shortcomings in the current tort system are such that even *The Washington Post* has noted that "the staggering costs and irrationality of America's civil justice system are unacceptable. The tort system is something of a casino, offering windfall judgments to a small number of claimants and nothing to others—with the merits of cases seeming almost irrelevant to their valuation."

Although each state faces its own set of challenges and problems, the medical liability crisis has nonetheless reached national proportions. Thus, we are grateful to have Dr. McClellan here to provide some insight into the problem and direction for reform.

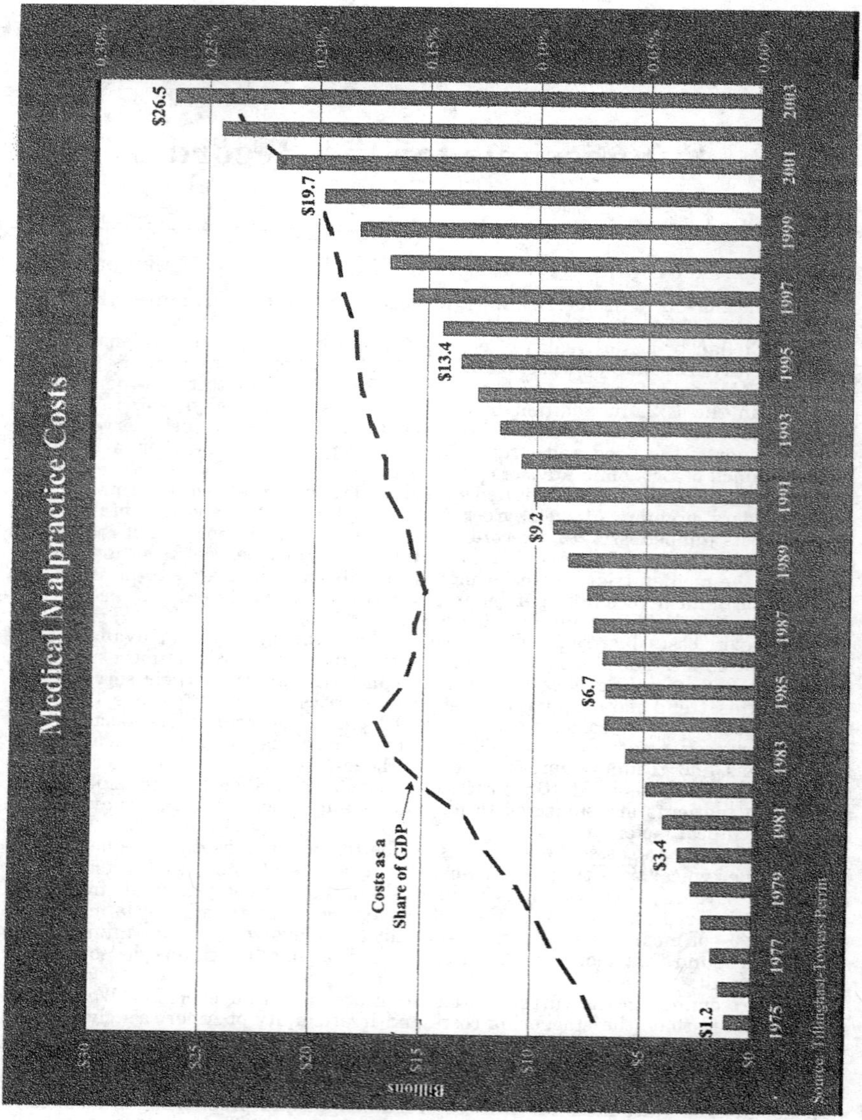
Medical Malpractice Costs
Billions
$30
$25
$20
$15
$10
$5
$0
0.30%
0.25%
0.20%
0.15%
0.10%
0.05%
0.00%
$1.2
$3.4
$6.7
$9.2
$13.4
$19.7
$26.5
Costs as a
Share of GDP
1975
1977
1979
1981
1983
1985
1987
1989
1991
1993
1995
1997
1999
2001
2003
Source: Tillinghast-Towers Perrin

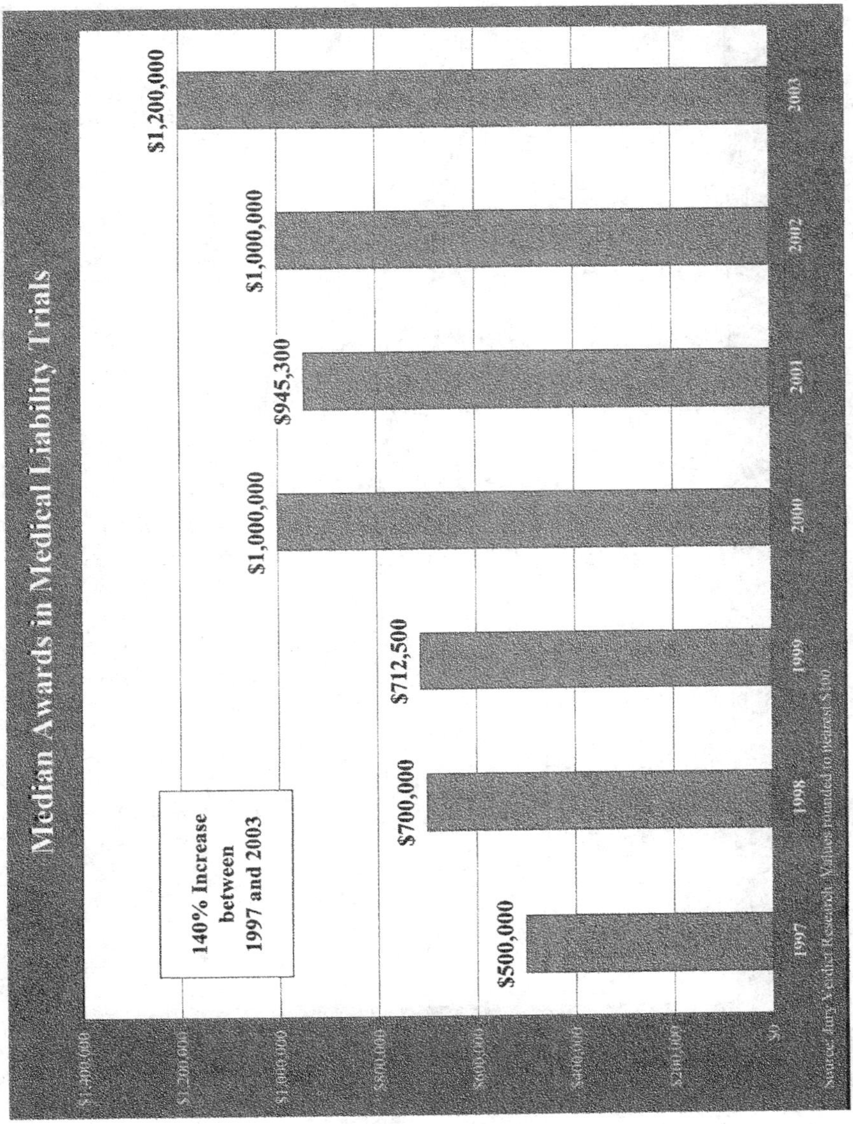

Median Awards in Medical Liability Trials
140% Increase
between
1997 and 2003
$500,000
$700,000
$712,500
$1,000,000
$945,300
$1,000,000
$1,200,000
$1,400,000
$1,200,000
$1,000,000
$800,000
$600,000
$400,000
$200,000
$0
1997
1998
1999
2000
2001
2002
2003
Source: Jury Verdict Research. Values rounded to nearest $100

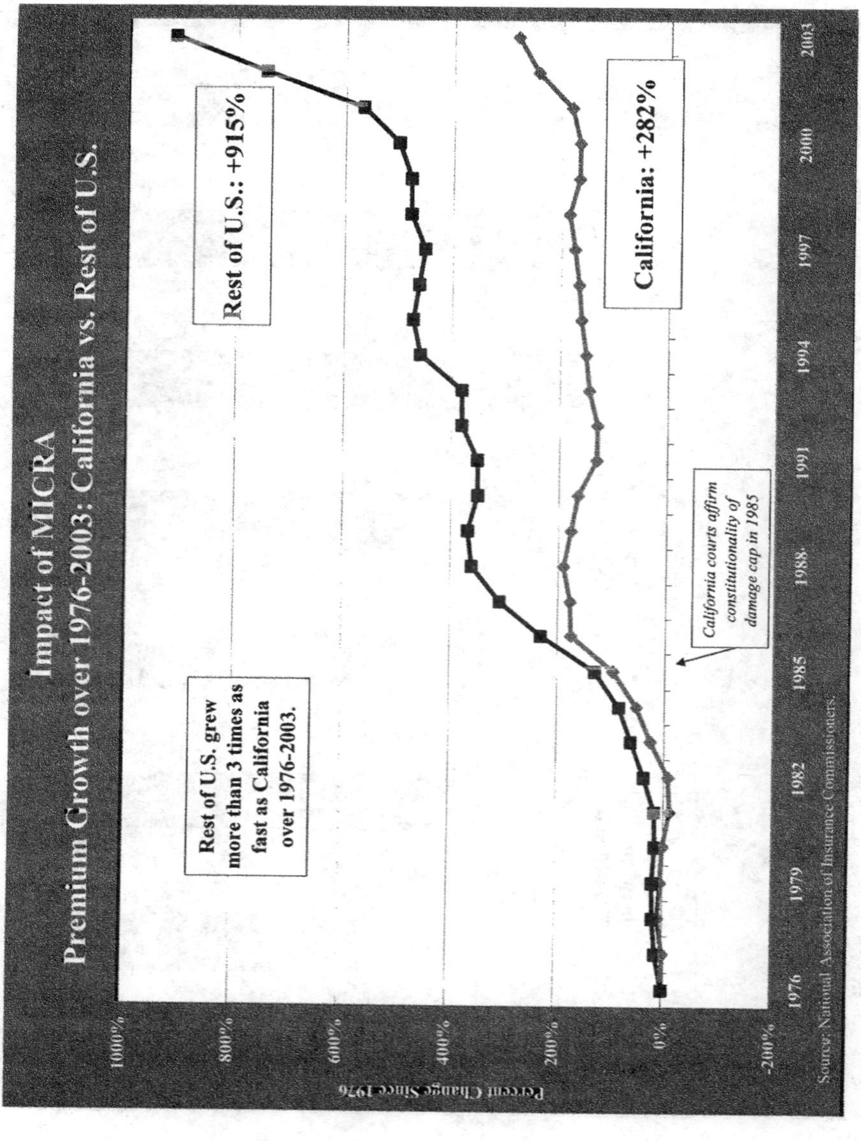

Impact of MICRA
Premium Growth over 1976-2003: California vs. Rest of U.S.
Rest of U.S.: +915%
Rest of U.S. grew more than 3 times as fast as California over 1976-2003.
California: +282%
California courts affirm constitutionality of damage cap in 1985
Percent Change Since 1976
1000%
800%
600%
400%
200%
0%
-200%
1976
1979
1982
1985
1988
1991
1994
1997
2000
2003
Source: National Association of Insurance Commissioners.

Impact of Caps on Non-Economic Damages

"Although experience varies across states, the data do indicate a long-term increase in awards and settlements per paid claim."

"The analysis indicates that capping payments from malpractice carriers was associated with lower premiums."

"Premiums in states with a cap on awards were 17.1 percent lower than in states without such caps. When using earned premium per physician as the dependent variable, the caps were associated with a 12 percent reduction in premiums."

Kenneth E. Thorpe

* Professor, Emory University School of Public Health
* Former Deputy Assistant Secretary for Health Policy, U.S. Department of Health and Human Services, in the Clinton Administration

Source: "The Medical Malpractice 'Crisis': Recent Trends and the Impact of State Tort Reforms," Health Affairs, *January 21, 2004*

America's Medical Liability Crisis: A National View

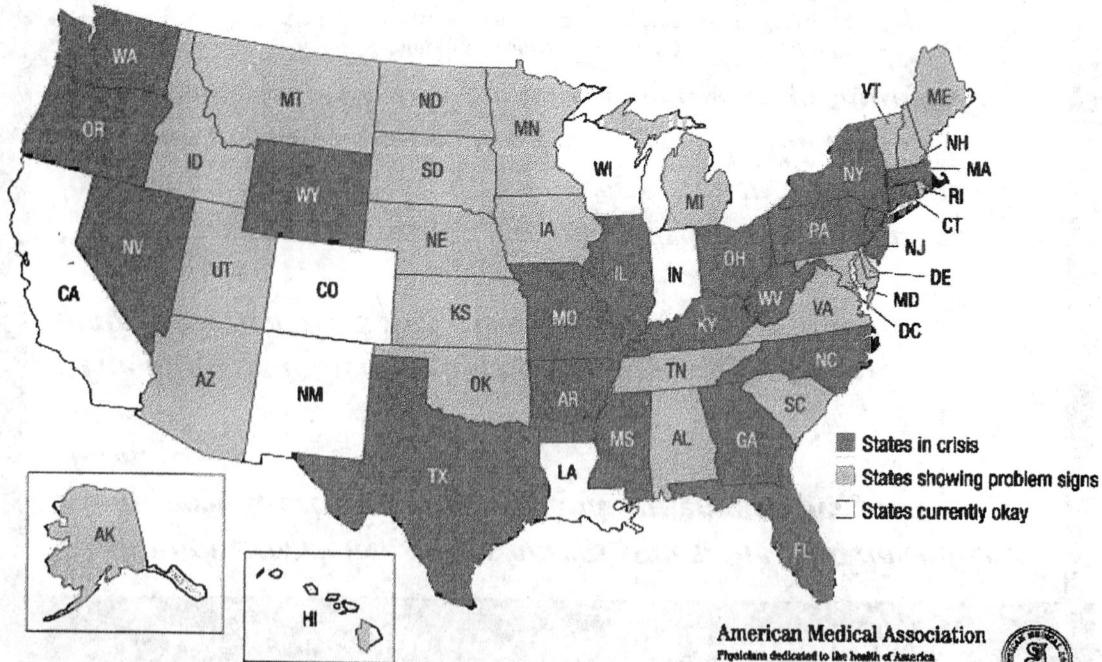

June 2004

American Medical Association
Physicians dedicated to the health of America

PREPARED STATEMENT OF SENATOR JACK REED, RANKING MINORITY MEMBER

Thank you, Chairman Saxton, for holding this hearing on an issue that has received a great deal of attention recently. l welcome Dr. McClellan and thank you for testifying today.

On the campaign trail last year, President Bush repeatedly criticized trial lawyers for filing "junk lawsuits" that he said were responsible for rising health ease costs. The centerpiece of the Administration's medical liability reform would cap non-economic damages at $250,000 and institute a three year statute of limitations on most lawsuits.

The 2004 Economic Report of the President stated that the President's reform plan would "lower the cost of providing health care." However, there's little, if any, evidence to support this claim. While it is certainly troubling that medical malpractice premiums for doctors have been rising rapidly in recent years, and many physicians in my state have informed me of the cost burden and the potential impact on access to care for patients, it is far from clear that jury awards are the sole driving force as the President suggests.

In 2003, the Government Accounting Office (GAO) studied states with and without caps on non-economic damages and found that the states with caps had lower premium increases than those without caps. However, GAO did not have enough data to show a direct link between malpractice award caps and premiums. Similarly, the Congressional Budget Office (CBO) has found that there are potential savings for malpractice premiums by limiting the amount of malpractice awards, but they are skeptical that a cap would provide relief for health care costs in general.

Malpractice costs were $24 billion in 2002, less than two percent of total national health care spending of $1.4 trillion, according to CBO. Reducing malpractice awards by 30 percent would only lower health care costs by approximately 0.5 percent or about $7 billion.

CBO also finds that limiting physicians' malpractice liability would have much impact on "defensive medicine" practices, such as providing unnecessary tests or procedures to avoid a lawsuit, because physicians do so more often out of concern for patients or to generate additional income than because they fear liability.

Dr. McClellan, I know you have studied the issue of defensive medicine and malpractice, so I will be particularly interested in your opinions about the amount of health cost savings non-economic caps on damages would produce.

I believe, however, that there are some other reasons for the latest increases in medical malpractice insurance premiums that would not be addressed by the kinds of reforms the President and his supporters are advocating. The GAO, for example, points to slower growth in insurance company investment income and reduced competition in the liability insurance market as other potential drivers behind rising malpractice premiums.

We also should not lose sight of the fact that this issue must be considered in the context of medical errors and the quality of patient care, which are inextricably linked to physician accountability. A study by the Institute of Medicine reported in 2000 that between 44,000 and 98,000 people die every year because of preventable medical errors. These statistics point to a need to link any discussion of tort reform to the issues of medical errors, public safety, and, physician accountability.

In the last Congress, the Republican leadership sent narrow medical liability legislation for OB/GYNs directly to the floor, thereby sidestepping serious Committee deliberation and inquiry into the nature of and possible solutions for rising insurance premiums. While it's hard to see how the President's proposal for medical liability reform will make more than a dent in spiraling health care costs; this is an important issue that lawmakers must be allowed to investigate thoroughly.

I appreciate Dr. McClellan's willingness to testify on this issue, but I also hope you will be open to questions regarding your oversight of the Centers for Medicare and Medicaid Services (CMS). I have a number of questions regarding the $500 billion of Federal spending that you administer at CMS that undoubtedly has a bigger impact on physician behavior and overall health spending than medical malpractice costs.

I look forward to Dr. McClellan's testimony.

PREPARED STATEMENT OF MARK MCCLELLAN, M.D., PH.D., ADMINISTRATOR, CENTERS FOR MEDICARE AND MEDICAID SERVICES

Chairman Saxton, Senator Bennett, distinguished members of the Committee, I thank you for inviting me here this morning to discuss the important topic of medical malpractice liability reform. It is a subject to which I have devoted considerable attention, both in my capacity as a civil servant and previously as an academic researcher and an internist. As President Bush and many in the Congress and across the country have recognized, our current malpractice liability system does not serve the needs of patients and is in need of reform. It is not simply an issue of lowering insurance premiums for physicians. It is particularly about patient safety and quality of care, as well as reducing unnecessary health care spending. According to the CBO, modification to malpractice laws will result in substantial savings to the Federal Government as a result of reduced malpractice premiums. My own research shows that resulting reductions in defensive medicine may also produce savings in both the public and private health care sector of up to several billion dollars per year.

All insurance programs are potentially subject to costs created by the liability environment. For example, a recent CMS letter to the Medicare Payment Advisory Commission (MedPAC) indicated that spending on physician services during 2004 rose by approximately 15 percent. A significant driver of this increase is the fact that more patients are receiving more complex and more frequent imaging services, such as magnetic resonance imaging and computer tomography scans. For several years now, in fact, spending for these diagnostic services has been rising at a more rapid rate than overall physician expenditures. Based on my own research and the research of many academic experts, my interactions with other physicians, and my experience as a clinician, it is clear to me that the practice of defensive medicine is contributing to these cost increases. The evidence suggests that reforms to the malpractice system, including caps on non-economic damages and revision of the joint and several liability rules can reduce defensive medicine, which can reduce unnecessary health care expenditures. The CBO scoring of legislation in 2003 estimated that Federal expenditures would drop by nearly $15 billion over ten years. Those savings depend only on reduced premiums. My own research concluded a reduction in defensive medicine could lower overall hospital expenditures by between five and nine percent. During FY 2004, the Medicare program spent more than $133 billion on hospital fee-for-service. That would mean potential annual savings of between $6.65 and $11.97 billion dollars, just for that program, not to mention the private sector.

Even more importantly, liability reforms will improve quality and access to health care, leading to better health for Americans. I would urge the Congress to work with the Administration to formulate a plan to address the problems with our current liability system and to promote a culture of patient safety and quality within the healthcare arena. The changes in liability law have the potential not only to produce significant savings, but also to simultaneously improve patient safety and the quality of care.

This morning I would like to review some of the systemic problems in medical malpractice liability and some innovative alternatives for addressing the needs of those who have been medically injured. Specifically, I would like to highlight the Department's "Early Offers" program as one possible way to speed resolution of malpractice claims so that patients' needs are satisfied in an effective, efficient manner.

THE CURRENT SYSTEM DOES NOT WORK

Malpractice liability laws seek to address two primary goals: first, to adequately compensate and care for the needs of patients who have been injured due to negligence, incompetence, or other improper conduct by a provider; and second, to motivate providers to engage in high quality, professional care. The existing system falls far short on both of these goals. The current judicial process for addressing malpractice needs to be reformed not simply to save money, but also because individuals who have just cause to make a claim are not receiving the help they need and deserve.

It is well known that the vast majority of individuals injured by a caregiver do not file suit. The 1990 Harvard Medical Practice study reported that only 2 percent of individuals experiencing an adverse event due to medical negligence filed suit and, of more concern, only 1 in 14 individuals seriously injured by such an event received any sort of compensation. More recent work by some of the same researchers confirms these findings.[1] The Physicians Insurance Association of America reports that, on average, it takes more than 5 years for an insurer to pay a malpractice claim after the date of the incident—mostly due to delays in reporting (22 months) and delays in the tort system (43 months). When an injured patient does finally successfully settle or win a case, lawyers typically take anywhere from 30–40 percent of those funds as compensation. In short, many of those who are injured due to negligent care are simply not receiving justice because the system does not work for them.

On the other side of the coin, the current system does not do much in terms of screening out cases with no medical merit, or in differentiating between adverse events due to negligence and unavoidable adverse events. A study published in the *New England Journal of Medicine* found "no association between the occurrence of an adverse event due to negligence or an adverse event of any type and payment . . . among the malpractice claims we studied, the severity of the patient's disability, not the occurrence of an adverse event or an adverse event due to negligence, was predictive of payment to the plaintiff.[2]

The same study reported that 10 of 24 cases involving no adverse event whatsoever were settled with a mean payment of nearly $29,000. Six of 13 cases involving an adverse event not due to negligence were settled with a mean payment of more than $98,000. More broadly, of claims filed during 2003, only about a third resulted in some payment to the plaintiff, and of the small percentage that go to trial, more than three in four resulted in a finding for the defendant, immediately leading one to question the validity of the bulk of claims.[3]

Rapidly rising premium rates can have a real impact on patient access to care. A study by the Agency for Healthcare Research and Quality examined how the supply of physicians varied across states between 1970 and the present. The study concluded that states adopting caps on non-economic damages experienced about 12 percent more growth in physicians per capita than States without caps. Notably, the study also found that States with relatively high caps were less likely to experience an increase in physician supply than States with lower caps.[4] This sort of disparity can translate into very real access challenges. It means that it is more difficult for patients to find the types of specialists they need, that they must go further out of their way, and take more time from their own lives to access the care they require. In some cases, the limitations on access result in negative health outcomes as well.

Just to illustrate, a 2004 survey of Ob/Gyns in Illinois found that in the previous two years, 11 percent had stopped practicing obstetrics as a result of medical liability concerns. Based on how many office visits physicians report in an average month (N=250), that means 46,250 office visits for Ob/Gyn services were lost across the state during those two years.

The malpractice system has important adverse effects on quality as well. In a widely read 1999 report, "To Err is Human," the Institute of Medicine (IOM) noted that: [R]eporting systems are an important part of improving patient safety and should be encouraged. These voluntary reporting systems [should] periodically assess whether additional efforts are needed to address gaps in information to improve patient safety and to encourage health care organizations to participate in. . .reporting, and track the development of new reporting systems as they form.[5]

The IOM emphasized that fear of lawsuits deters doctors and hospitals from making reports, even when they are not negligent, because in many states such reports can be used against them in court. This very understandable concern impedes quality improvement efforts. If our liability laws do not encourage error reporting and analysis, they serve only to perpetuate the very problems that they ostensibly exist to address.

The truth is that common human decency and professional ethics are sufficient motive for the vast majority of physicians to provide the best care possible. Most medical errors today are not the result of bad doctors or nurses, but rather the result of complex or difficult systems in which they work.

---

1 Studdert et al., Negligent Care and Malpractice Claiming Behavior in Utah and Colorado, Medical Care Vol. 38 No. 3 (2000), pp. 250–60.

2 Troyen A. Brennan, M.D., J.D., M.P.H., Colin M. Sox, B.A., and Helen R. Burstin, M.D., M.P.H., "Relation between Negligent Adverse Events and the Outcomes of Medical Malpractice Litigation," *The New England Journal of Medicine,* Volume 335: 1963–1967, December 26, 1996, Number 26.

3 Physician Insurers Association of America, "PIAA Claim Trend Analysis" 2003 ed. (2004).

4 Hellinger, Fred J., Ph.D., and William E. Encinosa, Ph.D., "Impact of State Laws Limiting Malpractice Awards on Geographic Distribution of Physicians," Agency for Healthcare Research and Quality, July 3, 2003.

5 Committee for Quality Health Care in America/Institute of Medicine, "To Err is Human: Building a Safer Health System," 2000.

You would think that we would do everything in our power to encourage the kind of self-analysis and systems evaluation necessary to identifying and addressing systemic errors. Instead, our current tort system sets up roadblocks that discourage this very important activity. This roadblock needs to be removed.

Congress should pass patient safety legislation that includes a mechanism for allowing anonymous reporting of errors and that protects databases of such information from discovery. If we don't collect this data, we'll never see the patterns that will allow us to make changes to improve patient safety and will never realize the concurrent savings resulting from reduced errors.

THE COSTS OF OUR CURRENT SYSTEM

As an acadmic, I conducted my own research on this subject that focused on whether, and to what extent, physicians engage in defensive medicine as a result of their concerns over being sued. In 1996, Stanford University Professor Daniel Kessler and I conducted a study on the extent to which physicians engage in defensive medicine.[6] We examined national data on Medicare beneficiaries experiencing a new primary diagnosis of serious cardiac illness in 1984, 1987, and 1990. We also compiled a comprehensive database of reforms to state liability laws and malpractice control policies from 1969 to 1992. Each of the observations in the Medicare data set was matched with a set of two tort law variables that indicated the presence or absence of direct or indirect malpractice reforms at the time of their initial hospitalization. Dr. Kessler and I found that direct liability reforms, such as caps on damage awards; abolition of punitive damages; and mandatory prejudgment interest and collateral-source rule reforms reduce hospital expenditures by 5 to 9 percent within 3 to 5 years of adoption. The drop in expenditures resulted from a change in physician practice patterns that we attributed to a moderation in defensive medicine. It is important to note that this shift had no consequence in terms of patient mortality or other serious adverse health events—that is, reforms made it possible to lower medical costs significantly without compromising quality of care. This particular study was peer reviewed and published in *The Quarterly Journal of Economics*. In 1997, the International Health Economics Association, a well-known global professional association of health economists, presented us with the Kenneth J. Arrow Award for this article.

The article's findings on the impacts of liability reforms on cost and quality are supported by a substantial body of other work. In an earlier study published in the *Journal of the American Medical Association*, researchers found a positive relationship between malpractice claims risk and rates of cesarean sections.[7] In a 2002 paper also published in a peer-reviewed economics journal, Dr. Kessler and I further explored the role of malpractice reforms in reducing defensive practices. Dr. Kessler and I found that malpractice reforms affect physician behavior by changing both financial measures of "malpractice pressure" (such as malpractice claims rates and malpractice insurance premiums) and non-financial measures (such as the time and hassle spent in defending against a claim). [8]

Based on the work we did, Dr. Kessler and I concluded that if direct liability reforms had been adopted nationwide between 1984 and 1990, it would have resulted in annual savings of $450 million for each of the first two years and close to $600 million for each of the succeeding years for *just the two conditions we studied.*[9] As I mentioned earlier, our study concluded that these reforms could potentially reduce overall hospital expenditures by five to nine percent. Those kinds of savings, if realized, could have a significant impact on the fiscal health of the Medicare and Medicaid programs. Furthermore, as stated above, these savings would come without any drop in the quality of care and outcomes experienced by patients.

CBO has taken issue with the estimates from the paper written by Dr. Kessler and me, contending that tort reform will not reduce defensive medicine. CBO used our work as a model, but their efforts are hampered by two critical methodological limitations. First, when CBO sought to replicate our study on a more recent sample of patients with the conditions we examined, it obtained similar results to ours. The finding of insignificant effects arose only when CBO sought to re-estimate our models on a set of patients with very broadly defined illnesses. Because hospital expend-

[6] Kessler, Daniel P. and Mark B. McClellan, "Do Doctors Practice Defensive Medicine?" *The Quarterly Journal of Economics,* vol. 111, no. 2, May 1996.

[7] Localio, Russell et al., Relationship Between Malpractice Claims in Cesarean Delivery, JAMA Vol. 269, January 20, 1993, p. 366.

[8] Kessler, Daniel P. and Mark B. McClellan, "How Liability Law Affects Medical Productivity," *Journal of Health Economics,* vol 21 (2002) pp. 931–55.

[9] Kessler, Daniel P. and Mark B. McClellan, "Do Doctors Practice Defensive Medicine?" *The Quarterly Journal of Economics,* vol. 111, no. 2, May 1996.

itures on patients with a broad range of illness are likely to be heterogeneous and hard to predict, the unexplained variance in hospital expenditures for these patients is likely to be large—larger than the unexplained variance in hospital expenditures for patients with clearly defined illnesses we studied. Since the standard errors of the estimates of the effects of limits on liability are proportional to the unexplained variance in expenditures, the statistical significance of estimates from models with broadly defined illnesses would be less than the significance of estimates from models with narrowly defined illnesses.

Second, we used more comprehensive data, while CBO used data from a 20 percent random sample of beneficiaries for most (1991–1996) of their study period. Third, there was very little variation in states' tort laws during the CBO's entire study period (1991–1999)—according to CBO staff, only 6 states changed one or the other of the two liability system variables under analysis. In the period that we studied (1984–1994), 33 states changed one or the other of the liability system variables under analysis. These two differences—the less comprehensive data and the smaller number of "experiments" in the CBO analysis—would also lead the statistical significance of estimates reported in their brief to be lower than the significance of our estimates.

It is important to put the differences between myself and Dr. Kessler, and the CBO, in the context of what we focused on. CBO has not made estimates of savings from reductions in defensive medicine. They have, however, concluded that reduced premiums would save the Federal Government billions of dollars. My own research shows the potential for billions more in savings as a result of reduce defensive medicine. What we both end up saying—along with numerous other researchers—is that reforms will lead to billions of dollars in savings each year.

LIABILITY CONCERNS REDUCE PHYSICIAN PRODUCTIVITY

Every time our malpractice system ties up a physician in judicial or administrative matters, then their clinical skills are temporarily removed from the productive pool. Even small drops in the average amount of time spent on malpractice claims will have the beneficial result of making physicians more productive in terms of patient care, which is ultimately where we want them to spend their time. The 2002 paper with Dr. Kessler that I mentioned, documented how this works: reform-induced decreases in the time and hassle spent defending against malpractice claims leads to lower health care costs, but not worse health outcomes.

The perceptions of practitioners themselves back up these statistical results. A 2002 poll by Harris Interactive found that the fear of litigation impacts healthcare administrative issues. Well over three-fourths of all physicians and nurses (84% and 81%, respectively) reported that they spend more time on paper work, such as medical record documentation, because of malpractice concerns than they would based solely on the patient's clinical needs. Additionally, nearly all physicians (94%) believe that written descriptions of cases are very often or sometimes influenced by the fear of litigation.[10]

In a 1997 paper, Dr. Kessler and I investigated how the intrusiveness of the liability system affected physician perceptions of medical care. We estimated the impact of liability reforms on objective measures of malpractice pressure—such as claims rates—and on perceptions of the effects of malpractice pressure on practice patterns. The study found that malpractice pressure affects physician perceptions of two important dimensions of medical practice: propensity to make referrals, and the ability to spend time with patients.[11]

More generally, the legalistic atmosphere in which physicians practice warps the physician-patient relationship. Hauser et al. give a good example of how fear of litigation can reduce the trust in the physician-patient relationship and actually become a barrier to clear and effective communication.

A woman went to a gynecologist for a problem and a minor surgical procedure was recommended. At the beginning of the discussion of this procedure, the physician commented, "The law requires me to inform you of certain facts about this operation." And then, in a perceptible alteration of his normal patterns of speech, the gynecologist began to chant a litany of side effects, risks, morbidity, mortality, percentages, probabilities, etc. The patient later reported that after about ten seconds of listening to this, her mind shut down entirely. "This appears to be some sort of

---

[10] Taylor, Humphrey, et. al., "Common Good Fear of Litigation Study: The Impact on Medicine," Harris Interactive, April 11, 2002.

[11] Kessler, Daniel and Mark McClellan, The Effects of Malpractice Pressure and Liability Reforms on Physicians Perceptions of Medical Care, Law and Contemporary Problems Vol. 60 (1997) pp. 81–106.

arcane ritual! The communication was not directed to me for any benefit of mine whatsoever.[12]

High-quality medicine requires effective communication with patients. The various tests and procedures available to us provide a tremendous amount of useful information, but often, a diagnosis, or the type of test to utilize, is prompted by something the patient shares with the physician in conversation. If, because of liability concerns, physicians are unable to discuss the inherent ambiguities and complexities of medical practice, and the variety of potential outcomes to a given procedure or service, in a manner to which the patient can personally relate, then the patient's ability to make informed decisions is compromised. Our current system, because it recasts this relationship in legalistic terms does not promote mutually beneficial exchanges of information.

INNOVATIVE PRIVATE SECTOR APPROACHES

Although those in the private sector cannot modify tort law, a number of organizations and providers have begun experimenting with mediation, with some success.

Some time ago, Johns Hopkins Hospital began requiring non-emergency patients who came to them for elective procedures (individuals who had the option of going elsewhere if they so chose) to sign an agreement to take any malpractice claims to mediation prior to going to court. In 2003, Hopkins mediated 24 cases and resolved 21 of them. As a result, Hopkins 2003 claims expenses decreased almost 30 percent. Mediation is typically much faster than a court case and involves far lower attorney's fees. In short, patients who are injured get compensated at a higher level and in a shorter amount of time. Furthermore, this reform has helped the hospital communicate more freely with the patients, and probably with the professional staff, in order to be sure the mediation is successful and the highest possible quality of care is achieved.

TORT REFORM AND LIABILITY INSURANCE PREMIUMS

As you are well aware, a fairly fierce debate over how the medical malpractice system should be reformed has been going on for some time now. While more research evidence would help in making the path forward obvious to all, there is no question that liability reform has the potential to produce significant healthcare savings, as well as reduce problems of access and quality care. The time to act on this issue is now—from the standpoint of health care quality and cost, we can't afford to wait.

A number of possibilities exist for improving our medical liability system. Tort reforms include actions such as capping awards for pain and suffering, so called non-economic damages, as well as capping punitive damages. In addition, suggestions have been made to reframe rules for joint and several liability, such that each actor involved in a given episode of care, including the physician, hospital, and payer, all bear a level of blame proportional to their share of fault or responsibility. Liability for damages would not be joint. As another option, attorneys' fees could also be capped, so that more of the dollars won by a plaintiff with a meritorious case actually go to that individual to address their health needs, and large awards could be paid as an annuity, or over a number of years, instead of as a lump sum, so that the money is available in the future when the individual needs it to pay for care. Collateral source rules, taking into account funds coming from health, automotive, or workers' compensation insurers, could also be modified to allow reductions in settlements or jury awards commensurate with insurers' payments. Alternatively, mandatory pre-trial screening by an independent medical expert to weed out baseless claims could reduce the number of baseless suits faced by physicians. President Bush supports securing the ability of injured patients to get fast, unlimited compensation for their economic losses, including the loss of ability to provide unpaid services like care for children or parents, but has urged the Congress to support a cap of $250,000 on non-economic damages, limit punitive damages, eliminate joint and severable liability, create a uniform statute of limitations, and provide for the structured payment of future damages.

According to the GAO, the greatest driver of increases in physician liability premium rates is losses suffered as a result of malpractice claims.[13] They also concluded that states with tort reforms that include certain damage caps had lower growth in liability premiums than did those without such caps. Another study by

---

[12] Hauser MJ, Commons ML, Bursztajn HJ, Gutheil TG. "Fear of Malpractice Liability and its Role in Clinical Decision Making," in *Gutheil TG, Bursztajn HJ, Brodsky A, Alexander,* v. *Decision Making in Psychiatry and the Law.* Baltimore: Williams & Wilkins, 1991.

[13] Hillman, p. 1.

Stephen Zuckerman et al. concluded that capping medical liability awards reduced premiums for general surgeons by 13 percent in the year following enactment of that reform and by 34 percent over the long term. The reforms resulted in similarly lower premiums for general practitioners and Ob/Gyns.[14] A 2002 HHS study found that during 2001, states with meaningful caps on non-economic damages saw average premium increases of 15 percent, while states without such caps saw increases of 44 percent.[15]

Like many academic studies, my own research has demonstrated that direct tort reform, including capping damages, abolition of mandatory prejudgment interest, and collateral source rule reforms reduce premium expenditures significantly. The 1997 paper with Dr. Kessler I mentioned above showed that in states adopting such reforms, within three years physicians saw substantially and statistically significant lower trend growth in their real malpractice insurance premiums of approximately 8.4 percent.[16]

Amounts paid on malpractice claims, either in settlement or because of a jury award, have been growing substantially in the past few years. The Physician Insurers Association of America (PIAA) reports that the median jury award in medical liability cases nearly doubled from 1997 to 2003, increasing from $157,000 to $300,000. The PIAA's as yet unpublished report on 2004 indicates that the median jury award during that year was $439,400; a one-year increase of more than 46 percent. It is notable that PIAA found a 2004 mean payment on a jury verdict of $606,907. Such a large difference between the median and the mean indicates the existence of a significant number of large awards. The size of settlements has similarly increased. Median settlements increased from $100,000 to $200,000 between 1997 and 2003. As previously noted, these increasing losses drive increases in premiums. However, physicians must also pay legal fees. Physicians who win at trial have average defense costs of $87,720 per claim and in cases where the claim was dropped or dismissed, their costs averaged $17,408.[17]

There is substantial evidence on the positive effects of tort reform to provide a basis for congressional action at this time. Not only will tort reform result in lower premiums, but, much more importantly, it will help foster an environment in which physicians do not feel the need to engage in defensive medicine and we will see our costs drop as a result. Tort reform will increase access to healthcare and it will result in improved quality as providers feel the freedom to openly discuss systemic improvements that will lead to a higher degree of patient safety. I would urge the Congress to take this issue up and act on it.

THE IMPACT OF MARKET FORCES

There is no significant controversy about whether the number of claims made against physicians and ballooning settlements and judgments has contributed to rising premiums. However, there are others who contend that the tort system itself is not the only reason for premiums to increase; they argue that the insurance market also contributes to the rise in premium rates.

Insurers typically invest the bulk of their revenues into bonds. Some people argue that during the stock market rise of the 1990s, insurers realized profits from their investments that allowed them to reduce premium rates. They contend that as the stock market has suffered declines, insurers have raised their premiums to make up for investment losses. In addition, many insurers purchase reinsurance from larger entities. Some say that such reinsurance has become increasingly expensive in the past few years, particularly after the tragedy on September 11, 2001, and that it is also common for insurers entering a new market to provide lower introductory rates in order to obtain market share, and then raise the rates once they have an established client base.

In addition to business cycle factors, the St. Paul Company, one of the larger physician insurers in the country, decided to cease providing malpractice coverage at the end of 2002. This action reduced competition among insurers and allowed them to, at least temporarily, increase their premium rates.

---

[14] Stephen Zuckerman, Randall R. Bovbjerg & Frank Sloan, "Effects of Tort Reforms and Other Factors on Medical Malpractice Insurance Premiums," 27 INQUIRY 167–182 (19.90).

[15] "Confronting the New Health Care Crisis: Improving Health Care Quality and Lowering Costs by Fixing our Medical Liability System," HHS Office of Assistant Secretary for Planning and Evaluation, July 24, 2002.

[16] Kessler, Daniel P. and Mark B. McClellan, "The Effects of Malpractice Pressure and Liability Reforms on Physicians' Perceptions of Medical Care."

[17] "Physician Insurers Association of America, "PIAA Claim Trend Analysis: 2003 ed. (2004).

Critics of tort reform efforts point to all of these factors as relevant to the malpractice debate. They argue that we should not engage in tort reform if it is not the only driver increasing premiums and expenditures.

The GAO concluded that although none of the companies it examined experienced a loss on their investments, a 1.6 percent decline in investment return from 2000 to 2002 would have resulted in premium increases of 7.2 percent over the same period.[18] Such a decline would not have been outside the realm of possibility given market movement during that period. Studies like these lend credence to the argument that a component of liability premium increases may result from factors other than rising settlements and jury awards.

That said, the present problem in many States is not the result of the so-called "insurance cycle," or reckless investments by insurance companies. Although we have been on an "up" part of the cycle, that does not explain extremely high premium increases in the last few years in some States that have not reformed their liability system, compared to much smaller increases in most of the States that have implemented significant reforms. The insurance cycle is not a phenomenon that occurs in some States but not others. But the growth in liability premiums and even the availability of liability insurance has clearly varied substantially across states, in association with differences in liability laws.

Consequently, reforms in insurance would not address the underlying causes of the problems of unnecessary costs, lower quality, and less access to care that result from our current liability system. Insurance market reforms will not change physicians' perception of the liability environment in which they work and market reforms will not reduce the level of defensive medicine. Furthermore, market based reforms will not produce swifter settlement of claims, or improve the equity of injured patients' compensation.

ADDITIONAL STEPS TO IMPROVE OUR LIABILITY SYSTEM

In late September of last year, then-Secretary Thompson announced an HHS initiative to deal with claims made against providers who are employees of the Department, including those practicing at community health centers or through Indian Health Service programs. To reduce the amount of time it takes a patient to receive compensation, HHS designed the Early Offers program to encourage rapid settlement of cases, provide quick payment in deserving cases, and avoid the delay, cost, and emotional distress of litigation.

When a patient who has been served at a federally-funded health center or Indian Health Center facility files a medical malpractice liability claim against HHS, we send a standard notice explaining our early offers program. Both sides have 90 days to submit a confidential offer to a neutral third party who will compare the offers and notify both sides only if a match is made. Not only are offers voluntary, their amount and existence remain confidential forever if no match is made. So neither side tips its hand or loses leverage if the case goes to court.

The program is up and running at HHS and we're hopeful that it will show promising results in the months to come. In the meantime, any doctor or hospital can set up an early offers program. Because an early settlement only occurs when both parties agree, you're not losing any options by setting up a program, and no government action is required.

Evidence on how we can improve quality of care for patients should drive our reform efforts. We should be sure that if doctors take steps to encourage quality, for example, installing and using electronic medical records so that they can more easily track adverse events and thereby prevent them, that these physicians are not then punished by our legal system. If a physician who is considering such a system has in the back of his/her mind the fact that some day an attorney might use his data to bring suit, that physician may abandon the idea altogether. We should be looking to create systems that support quality care, that provide the data that are needed for good decision making.

To illustrate what can happen when physicians are able to be more open with their patients about medical errors, I would point you to the experience of the Lexington, Kentucky Veterans Affairs medical center. In 1987, after losing two malpractice cases with judgment totaling more than $1.5 million, this facility adopted a policy of radical honesty. They began to openly and immediately discuss with patients and/or their families any errors that occurred during treatment, including giving the patient information about their right to file a claim or an application for compensation. Furthermore, the facility disclosed medical errors when the patient or family had no reason to know one had occurred. A 1999 study of the Lexington

[18] Hillman, p. 8.

facility's claims experience during the years 1990 to 1996 concluded that the facility did not pay any more in malpractice claims than comparable VA facilities, and had concurrently avoided significant legal expenditures.[19] Partially due to the success of the Lexington policy, the VA adopted this practice system-wide in 1995.

The VA is not entirely analogous to the private market, but I bring up this example because it demonstrates how the real needs of patients who have been injured can be addressed more adequately when systems are in place to encourage patient-physician communication.

CONCLUSION

We are considering a variety of administrative ways to test innovative ideas that would lead to a solution to the malpractice problem.

Mr. Chairman, the current medical liability system simply does not address the needs of patients, and it's costing those patients, the Federal Government, and other payers billions of dollars every year because it adds to costs and encourages care that does not improve health. More importantly, our liability system reduces access and reduces quality of care. I would encourage the Congress to take action on this issue and would be happy to work with you as you move forward. I would be pleased to take any questions at this time.

[19] Kraman, Steve S. and Ginny Hamm, "Risk Management: Extreme Honesty May be the Best Policy," in *Annals of Internal Medicine,* vol. 131, issue 12, 21 December 1999, pp. 963–67.

DEPARTMENT OF HEALTH & HUMAN SERVICES
Centers for Medicare & Medicaid Services
7500 Security Boulevard, Mail Stop N3-01-21
Baltimore, Maryland 21244-1850

CMS
CENTERS for MEDICARE & MEDICAID SERVICES

Office of the Actuary

DATE: February 11, 2005

FROM: Richard S. Foster
Chief Actuary

TO: Mark B. McClellan, M.D., Ph.D.
Administrator

SUBJECT: Effectiveness of Drug Price Negotiations by the Federal Government versus Medicare Prescription Drug Plans

Under the Medicare Modernization Act (P.L. 108-173), the new Medicare prescription drug benefit will be provided through private health insurance organizations. In general, health plans that can negotiate favorable retail drug price discounts and drug manufacturer rebates, and take other steps to manage utilization and costs effectively, will be able to offer lower premiums to beneficiaries. Prescription drug plans that are effective in these efforts can gain a competitive advantage over other plans.

We have estimated that Medicare prescription drug plans can initially achieve an average cost reduction of 15 percent (compared to retail-level, unmanaged prescription drug costs), with this reduction increasing to 25 percent over a 5-year period.[1] The ultimate savings level of 25 percent has frequently been achieved in practice by pharmacy benefit managers on behalf of large drug insurance plans. These savings assumptions were reviewed in 2004 by an independent panel of expert health actuaries and economists. The panel found the assumptions to be reasonable and did not recommend any changes to them.

Under section 1860D-11(i) of the Social Security Act, as added by the Medicare Modernization Act, the Secretary of Health and Human Services is prohibited from participating in the drug price negotiations conducted by Medicare prescription drug plans with drug manufacturers and pharmacies. Similarly, the Secretary cannot establish a price structure for reimbursing covered Part D drugs. The question has arisen as to whether allowing such a role for the Secretary could produce greater cost reductions than the negotiations of individual Medicare prescription drug plans.

[1] These estimated cost reductions reflect the combined effect of retail price discounts, manufacturer rebates, and utilization-management programs.

My staff and I have not prepared a formal estimate of the impact of eliminating section 1860D-11(i). We have informally considered the issue and have reached the following tentative conclusions:

- As noted above, Medicare prescription drug plans will have a strong incentive to negotiate effective price reductions. Pharmacy benefit managers have had substantial experience with such efforts and have demonstrated their effectiveness for many years.

- The Secretary's ability to achieve price reductions would depend on the Federal government's willingness to use its large-purchaser power in a forceful way. At one extreme, the Secretary could virtually dictate price levels to manufacturers and retail pharmacies. In theory, such a practice could result in very large discounts, well in excess of our expected levels under the MMA. In practice, however, it is not clear that manufacturers and pharmacies would be willing to sell prescription drugs at very low prices mandated in this fashion. Moreover, we do not believe that the current Administration or future ones would be willing and able to impose price concessions that significantly exceed those that can be achieved in a competitive market.

- Establishment of drug price levels for Medicare by the Federal government would eliminate the largest factor that prescription drug plans could otherwise use to compete against each other. This change would have implications for the degree of competition in the Medicare prescription drug plan market, by reducing the premium differentials among plans. Lower premium differentials would reduce beneficiaries' incentives to select a lower-cost drug plan.

- The past experience of Congress and the Medicare program in regulating drug prices has not been reassuring. A well-known example is the Part B covered drugs. Prior to the MMA, these drugs were reimbursed at rates that, in many instances, were substantially greater than prevailing price levels.

In considering these issues, we believe that direct price negotiation by the Secretary would be unlikely to achieve prescription drug discounts of greater magnitude than those negotiated by Medicare prescription drug plans responding to competitive forces. Please let us know if you have any questions about this information.

Richard S. Foster, F.S.A.
Chief Actuary

Securing the Benefits of Medical Innovation for Seniors: The Role of Prescription Drugs and Drug Coverage

U.S. Department of Health and Human Services
Office of the Assistant Secretary for Planning and Evaluation
July, 2002

EXECUTIVE SUMMARY

Americans are living longer and healthier lives. By the year 2030, the number of Americans over the age of 65 is projected to double to 70 million. The life expectancy of the average American is increasing, and the rates of mortality, morbidity, and disability among Americans over age 65 have steadily decreased. In the past, aging has been associated with the development of chronic medical conditions, such as cancer, arthritis, diabetes, and heart disease, which limit participation in daily activities and reduce the quality of life. However, recent advances in the prevention and treatment of chronic diseases have radically altered the quality of life for older Americans.

Innovations in medical science, especially pharmaceuticals, have shifted the focus of medicine from highly invasive treatments and surgeries with potentially serious risks to less-invasive therapies focused on prevention and health maintenance. This shift has allowed many older Americans to remain healthy and independent, avoiding long hospital or nursing home stays. As a result, the Baby Boom and subsequent generations of seniors will likely live longer, healthier, and more productive lives.

The future of medical innovations appears to be even more promising. Many scientists believe that we are on the verge of another round of significant breakthroughs in medical research and development due to the recent mapping of the human genome. The rapidly evolving field of genetic medicine will provide researchers with many new targets for future drug development, as well as provide doctors with information about how to more effectively treat chronic medical conditions. In fact, as a result of pharmacogenomics, physicians may be able to select drugs that are ideally suited for individual patients based on their genetic makeup.

However, the development of valuable new treatments is often costly and time consuming. Consequently, continued investment in research and development is critical to ensure that new treatments are available to enrich the lives of tomorrow's seniors. Both public and private sector efforts are required to maintain a full 'pipeline' of medical innovations.

The United States plays a vital role in the global development of new pharmaceutical treatments, leading the world in spending for research and development of new drugs and biologics and in the introduction and sale of major innovative new drug products. The U.S. leadership in medical innovation and in the availability of valuable new treatments is directly related to the U.S. reliance on competitive approaches in health insurance coverage to encourage medical innovations and reduce costs. For non-elderly Americans, private health insurance plans in the United States use competitive tools like volume purchasing and disease management programs to reduce drug costs. In contrast, many countries rely on direct government controls to keep costs down. These countries seek to reduce drug spending by using the government's authority to delay or deny regulatory approvals or insurance coverage for new medicines, or to restrict coverage significantly for approved drugs (see appendix). These countries can do so because, in contrast to the United States, most health care is delivered through health insurance plans where the government can restrict coverage and availability of therapies.

For example, patients in some countries face restrictions on access to newer drugs (bisphosphonates) that are more effective and have fewer side effects compared to alternatives (e.g., hormone replacement therapies) in treating older women and others at risk of osteoporosis. Osteoporosis is associated with a significant risk of serious fractures, including hip fractures. In some countries, individuals must have conclusive evidence of low bone density, the hallmark of osteoporosis, or must actually have experienced an osteoporotic fracture before reimbursement for these newer agents is permitted.

As another example, several countries deny reimbursement for a new treatment of asthma—Singulair® (montelukast). This treatment provides for good control of asthma, reducing the need for steroid therapy. Although steroids are a standard treatment for asthma, they may induce significant side effects in individuals who require their long-term use.

This report demonstrates the potentially serious consequences to medical innovation and overall health posed by attempts to contain drug expenditures by implementing government controls that are inevitably arbitrary and out of touch with the diversity of patient needs and circumstances. If applied broadly in the United States, government-controlled restrictions on the coverage of new drugs could put the future of medical innovation at risk and may retard advances in treatment and in the development and introduction of new products. Moreover, government controls may reduce or delay access to specific drugs for seniors. Even when a drug is available, government controls often increase the likelihood that older, lower cost products will be prescribed rather than newer, more innovative products, which may have fewer side effects or other features that improve patient compliance and hence, the effectiveness of medical treatment.

In contrast to many other countries, the U.S. market is relatively free of government-controlled programs to contain medical costs. Although participation in many federal and state buying programs may require certain types of controls—such as rebates and coverage limits—these programs represent only a small fraction of the market.

To ensure continued progress in the fight to treat and prevent diseases, especially the chronic illnesses of older age for which we may be on the verge of unprecedented breakthroughs, the American health care system should not resort to government controlled drug coverage decisions. Other steps can and should be taken to reduce the costs of drugs, such as investing in biomedical research on less costly and more effective treatments, protecting the intellectual property rights of American companies worldwide, improving the efficiency of the regulatory process for new treatments, and increasing the availability and effectiveness of competitive approaches to limit the cost of new treatments. These steps will help keep drugs available and affordable without reducing access to valuable new treatments and discouraging innovation just at the time when the potential for innovation is greatest.

INTRODUCTION

Americans are living longer and healthier lives.

- By the year 2030, the percentage of Americans over the age of 65 will grow dramatically, doubling in number to 70 million (almost 20% of the U.S. population).
- Since 1900, the life expectancy of the average American has increased 29 years. (CDC 2002)
- Over the past century, and especially in the 1980s and 1990s, the rates of mortality, morbidity, and disability among Americans over age 65 have steadily decreased. (CDC 2001; Freedman 2002)
- A recent report by the Centers for Disease Control and Prevention (CDC) notes that between 1979-81 and 1995-97, death rates declined six percent in women and 19 percent in men ages 65 to 74, and eight percent in women and 16 percent in men ages 75 to 84.
- The world's population is aging, too. In the next 50 years, the median age of the world's population will increase 10 years. (United Nations 2002)
- Many of the gains in longevity and quality of life are directly related to advances in medical science and technology, including pharmaceuticals. One new study found that half the drugs prescribed or administered in office visits in 1999 were not prescribed or administered at all in 1985. (Burt 2002)

Percentage of the U.S. Population Age 65 and Older, 1900 to 2050

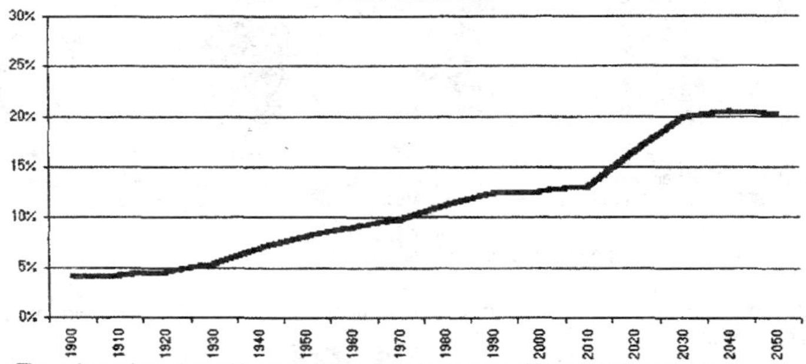

Note: These data refer to the resident population. Data for the years 2000 to 2050 are middle-series projections of the population.
Source: U.S. Census Bureau, Decennial Census Data and Population Projections

In the past, aging has been associated with the development of chronic medical conditions, such as cancer, arthritis, diabetes, and heart disease, which limit participation in daily activities and reduce the quality of life. However, recent advances in the prevention and treatment of chronic diseases have radically altered the quality of life for older Americans. As a result, the Baby Boom and subsequent generations of seniors will likely live longer, healthier, and more productive lives.

The CDC cites decreases in deaths from cardiovascular disease, atherosclerosis, cancer, and hypertension as key contributors to the overall decline in mortality. (CDC, NCHS March 2001) Other studies have found that the levels of physical and cognitive disability among older Americans declined during the 1990s, suggesting that seniors are healthier, and more productive and independent than they were just a decade ago. (Federal Interagency Forum on Aging-Related Statistics 2002; Freedman 2002, 2000, 1998)

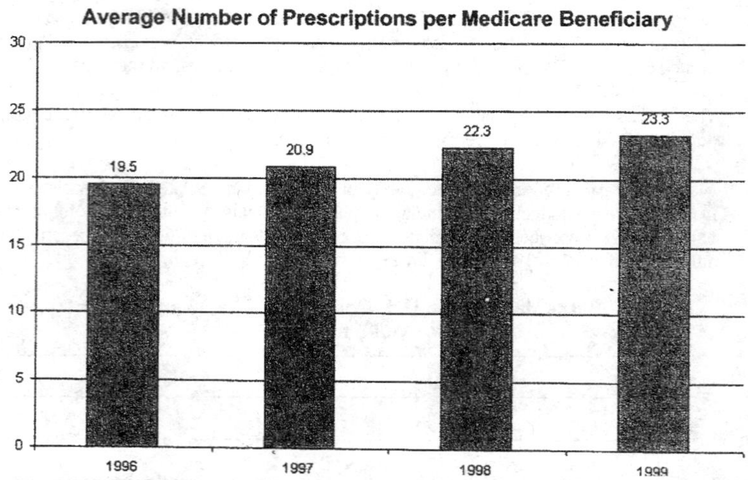

Note: The MCBS is believed to under-report the number of prescriptions received by Medicare beneficiaries.
Source: 1999 Medicare Current Beneficiary Survey (MCBS), non-institutionalized population only.

Medical innovations are critical to seniors' quality of life.

Health experts point to advances in disease treatment and prevention as key factors in improving the health of older Americans.

- In recent years, new drugs, medical procedures, screening tools, and prevention strategies have improved the treatment of chronic diseases, which affect 80 percent of all seniors. (CDC, NCCDPHP 1999)

- Prescription drug use has dramatically increased in seniors, indicating that many are taking advantage of new medicines to improve their health and quality of life.

Over the past century, medical innovations, including new drugs, have altered not only the health status of Americans, but also the basic pattern of life in America and around the world:

- Antibiotics and vaccines have drastically reduced the burden of infectious disease in America.

- Readily available insulin transformed type 1 diabetes from a childhood death sentence to a chronic but manageable disease.

- Gastric acid reducing agents, such as H2 blockers, revolutionized the treatment of gastric ulcers by eliminating the need for surgery.

- Effective, tolerable psychiatric medications have made it possible for millions of Americans to lead normal lives, free from the extreme suffering caused by mental illness.

- New technologies (such as coronary angioplasty, pacemakers, and cardiac stents) have enhanced quality of life among those suffering with chronic heart disease.

Often, the benefits from development of new drugs and technologies are additive. For example, a host of medical advances have combined to yield a 35 percent reduction in mortality from coronary heart disease and a 36 percent reduction in mortality from stroke since 1980. (See Chart 3)

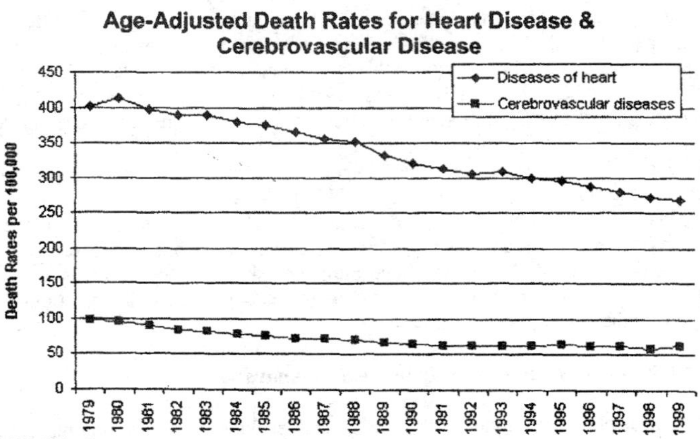

Source: Vital Statistics Data, NCHS

In addition to providing cures and preventing more severe and costly effects of diseases, innovations in treatment and medical science, especially pharmaceuticals, have shifted the focus of medicine from highly invasive treatments and surgeries with potentially serious risks to less-invasive practices and therapies focused on prevention and health maintenance. This shift has allowed many older Americans to remain healthy and independent, avoiding long hospital or nursing home stays.

The future of medical innovation looks promising.

- The recent mapping of the human genome may usher in a new era of medical therapeutics.

- Future generations of American seniors stand to benefit from continued vigorous medical innovation.

Many scientists believe that we are on the verge of another significant round of breakthroughs in medical research and development due to the recent mapping of the human genome. The deciphering of the human genome has improved our understanding of health and disease. (Bumol 2001) As scientists learn more about the function of different genes and their protein products, we will gain a more sophisticated knowledge of the cellular and molecular mechanisms of specific diseases. At the same time, new biological techniques and tools will enable scientists to explore both normal and abnormal biological systems with high molecular resolution.

As a result, pharmaceutical research will be able to capitalize on this increased appreciation of the cellular and molecular basis for diseases by identifying new genetic or protein targets for drug development. New products will be designed to interact with specific molecular entities involved in the generation of certain diseases. This targeted approach may reduce disabling or complicating side effects, which limit the usefulness of some current treatments. For example, new cancer treatments are being developed that target specific molecular features of cancer cells not found in normal cells. Hence, these agents will attack cancer cells but not healthy cells, thereby reducing some of the debilitating side effects of more standard cancer chemotherapy.

In the future, advances in genetic medicine may permit pharmaceutical therapy based on an individual's unique genetic map. The evolving field of pharmacogenomics will allow physicians to select drugs that are ideally suited for individual patients based on their genetic makeup. (Weinstein 2000) Again, this approach may improve the efficiency and minimize the side effects of disease treatment. Moreover, determining the risk of developing a disease based on the genetic profile of asymptomatic patients may permit early preventive interventions that will delay or prevent the development of diseases.

The United States provides leadership in medical innovation

The United States plays a prominent role in the global development of new pharmaceuticals.

- The U.S. leads the world in spending for research and development of new drugs and biologics. (Gambardella 2001)

- The National Institutes of Health budget for Fiscal Year 2002 is $23.5 billion.
- Six of the world's top ten pharmaceutical companies are headquartered in the United States. (Gambardella 2001)
- The Food and Drug Administration is recognized worldwide as setting the gold-standard for quality and timely review of new drugs and biologics.
- As a result of investment in research and development, U.S. pharmaceutical companies lead the world in the introduction and sale of major innovative products.

National Institutes of Health Budget

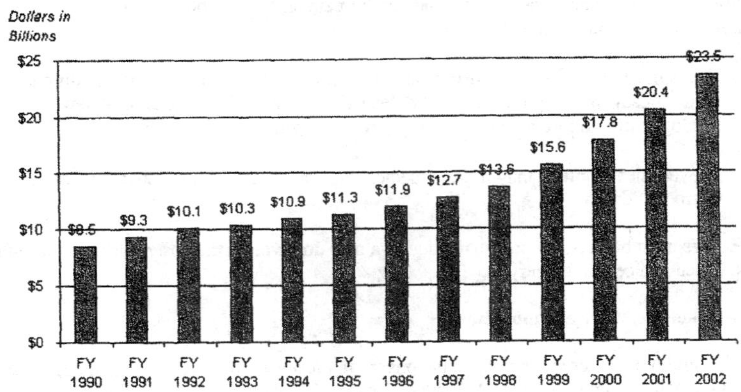

Most of the basic research on new drugs is concentrated in a few areas of the world—namely the United States, Europe, and Japan. (United States International Trade Commission 2000) Clinical trials occur in almost every country. As reported by the United States International Trade Commission (USITC), the U.S. accounted for 45 percent of 152 globally-marketed products developed from 1975 to 1994; followed by the UK at 14 percent; Germany, 7 percent; Japan, 7 percent; and France, 3 percent. Therefore, in the past, the U.S. public and private sectors have shouldered much of the cost for research and development of new products.

Robust investment in research and development by the United States has resulted in U.S. dominance of global sales of new pharmaceuticals. In the 1990's, sales of major innovative products by U.S. multinational pharmaceutical companies increased more significantly than those of their European counterparts. (Gambardella 2001) Specifically, the U.S. share of sales of new chemical entities (drugs whose active ingredients have not been previously approved for therapeutic use) launched during the 1990's approached 70 percent. (Gambardella 2001)

Moreover, in 1999, more than 80% of total sales of the world's top 15 drugs were produced by U.S. companies. (Gambardella 2001)

Future innovations will continue to improve the health and lives of older Americans and revolutionize the treatment of chronic disease. However, since the development of new technologies may take years, continued investment in research and development is critical to ensure that new treatments are available to enrich the lives of tomorrow's seniors. Both public and private sector efforts are required to maintain a full 'pipeline' of medical innovations.

FACTORS INFLUENCING MEDICAL INNOVATION

Multiple factors influence whether new and better treatments for chronic diseases will be available for current and future generations.

- Investment in biomedical research, an efficient regulatory process to assure drug safety and efficacy, patent protection of intellectual property, and fair pricing of new drugs and biologics are important elements to ensure continued medical innovation.

- Government controls may impede medical innovation and new product development and introduction.

Developers must balance the potential value of a new drug versus the cost of bringing it to the marketplace in a certain country.

The Market for Medical Innovation

The U.S. and most other industrialized nations try to create environments that will encourage innovation and research for cures of dreaded diseases. One of the most important ways nations do that is through a system of patents and other intellectual property rights that provide incentives for individuals to perform such research. Patents grant exclusive property rights to the innovator for a limited number of years. Thus, the patent system encourages creativity and investment in innovations. [World Intellectual Property Organization (WIPO) 2002] The period of market exclusivity allows pharmaceutical companies to recapture some of their investment costs. After a patent expires, less expensive generic products can be produced and sold in the marketplace, effectively competing with brand name drugs. Since patents are granted on a territorial basis, inventors (pharmaceutical companies) must apply for a patent in each country or state separately. As a result, not all innovations are patented in every country. Moreover, some countries deem certain products, including drugs, exempt entirely from patent protection. (WIPO 2002)

Patent policy inevitably affects how much money investors will gamble on research and development of new pharmaceuticals. Moreover, patent policy potentially influences the categories or types of diseases for which pharmacological treatments are sought. Pharmaceutical companies will be more apt to develop treatments for diseases that have a relatively high prevalence in the population. (WIPO 2002)

The tenure of a patent will affect the ability of a pharmaceutical company to recoup its investment and finance development of new products. In the United States the term of patent protection is 20 years. However, the effective patent term—the time remaining after a product has gained market approval—for a specific product may be less, depending on the time it takes to bring that product to the market. Other countries may have different patent terms, which may further limit the period of effective market exclusivity. (USITC 2000) Over the last two decades, the duration of patent exclusivity among different countries has been converging, although some differences remain. Patent restoration laws have restored some of the erosion in the period of exclusivity.

At the same time, for diseases with relatively low prevalence in the population, other governmental policies can provide the necessary incentives for drug research and development where the market may not. The U.S. Orphan Drug Act of 1983, for example, has been successful at stimulating research and development on rare diseases by awarding market exclusivity to the developer of the first drug for a condition unless subsequent drugs are clinically superior. (Kremer 2000)

Access to Medical Innovation

Before a new drug can be marketed, it must pass rigorous regulatory scrutiny. The purpose of the regulatory process is, correctly, to ensure that marketed drugs are safe and efficacious for patients. Most countries have a governmental body that is charged with approving and regulating new drugs. Regulators in different countries have an impact on the development and testing of drugs, advertising, and, in some cases, the pricing and delivery of products (see below). (USITC 2000) Regulatory requirements can expedite and facilitate or, conversely, prevent or delay a drug's introduction into the marketplace. Delays in marketing will deprive individuals from receiving new drugs, which may impact both longevity and quality of life. Moreover, if a nation's regulatory process is too restrictive, a pharmaceutical company may decide to forgo seeking approval for its drug in that country completely.

Efforts to expedite the drug review process have allowed patients more timely access to new pharmaceuticals. For example, dramatic improvements in efficiency of FDA pre-market review, following the 1992 enactment and reauthorization of the Prescription Drug User Fee Act (PDUFA), have cut review time in half. With a "priority" review process, thousands of cancer patients in the U.S. have had earlier access to new cancer treatments. This in turn has extended many cancer patients' lives, or improved their quality of life. For example, a new biologic for the treatment of breast cancer (Herceptin®/trastuzumab) was approved by the FDA in less than five months. This drug took 18 months to be approved in Europe. An estimated additional 10,000 American women with advanced breast cancer received this new treatment as a result of the timely review process. This added an estimated 2,300 years of life to the population who had access to this new treatment following its market approval in May 1998.

With other new treatments, an expedited review process has helped thousands of patients to avoid significant sickness and hospitalization. For example, a six-month review and approval of a new treatment for osteoporosis (Fosamax®/alendronate sodium) is estimated to have allowed thousands of women earlier access to this treatment, preventing as many as 3,000 hip and wrist fractures. The accompanying shift in worldwide drug research and development investments toward the U.S. has prompted the European authority to consider emulating the FDA's process, including a "priority" review for important new drugs.

Recently, the European Commission (EC) recognized the deleterious effects of delays brought on by bureaucratic drug restrictions. An EC advisory panel noted that "[t]he [pharmaceutical] price negotiating systems and reimbursement structures in a number of Member States can lead to significant delays. This is not only a problem within those Member States, but it can also result in citizens of one Member State having access to medicines months, or even years, in advance of those in other Member States." (European Commission, 2002) One study of the European drug market found that for 22 breakthrough drugs (new molecular entities, or NMEs), it could take up to four years between the time the drug was first available anywhere in Europe and the time it was available in all the countries studied. The average delay was over two years. (Europe Economics 2000)

Cost containment efforts may reduce or delay access to specific drugs. In contrast to the U.S., where individuals generally may obtain any approved product on the market, in other countries, governmental policy may limit the use of a drug to specified categories of patients or restrict its use entirely. Even when a drug is widely available, government cost-containment programs may result in an increased likelihood that older, lower-cost products will be prescribed rather than newer, more innovative products. (USITC 2000) Although generic alternatives may work just as well and may be cost saving, health care providers rather than government officials should retain the decision-making authority regarding the best treatment option for individual patients.

Many countries attempt to control public expenditures for drugs by allowing the government to influence drug pricing and coverage decisions directly. In fact, the U.S. is the only major industrialized country that does not impose some general form of government controls on insurance coverage of prescription drugs. (Calfee 2000) Approaches used by various countries include direct and indirect price controls, profit controls, reference pricing, physician budget constraints, and copayment programs. (USITC 2000) The governments enforce these controls through their ability to influence which drugs are covered for all or most of their citizens—an authority that the U.S. government has never generally had. Thus, foreign governments have the authority to restrict coverage of certain drugs to limit pharmaceutical expenditures, even when drugs prove cost-effective over other treatment options. (USITC 2000; Lichtenberg 2001; Neumann 2000; Cutler 2001)

The desire of countries to control health spending is certainly understandable. Moreover, levels of U.S. prescription drug spending have unambiguously increased in recent years due to increases in both the number of prescriptions and prices. For most of the U.S. prescription drug market, rising costs have driven employers and insurers to adopt various market-based techniques of cost containment, largely free of government intervention. Techniques such as tiered formularies, step therapy, coinsurance rather than fixed copayments, and generic substitution— with appropriate regulatory mechanisms to ensure patient safety— have kept prescription drug coverage within the reach of most Americans. Most Americans with private insurance, or the employers and others purchasing insurance on their behalf, also have choices about coverage that are not available in the government-controlled health financing plans of other countries—so that if an insurance plan does not provide appropriate coverage for valuable treatments, individuals in the U.S. can go elsewhere for coverage. Drugs that the FDA has approved as safe and efficacious are widely available for sale when needed. At the same time, changes in U.S. drug purchasing and distribution have stimulated competition and, indirectly, encouraged innovation. (Gambardella 2001) Only 13 percent of the U.S. market is covered by Medicaid or other public programs that use direct government controls to limit costs. (USITC 2000)

Cost-containment approaches implemented by individual countries may have a significant impact on prescription drug innovation, especially in regard to essential research and development expenditures. (USITC 2000) Government controls on drug access and pricing may result in decreased revenues, which reduce monies available for research and development. (USITC 2000). As a result of reduced investment in research and development, innovation may be slowed, delaying the development and introduction of new drugs into the marketplace. Partially as a result of various administered pricing schemes, Europe seriously lags behind the U.S. in drug research, and the gap is widening. In 1990, major European research-based pharmaceutical companies spent 73 percent of their R&D budget in Europe. By 1999, they spent only 59 percent in Europe, moving most of it to the U.S. (Gambardella 2001) One recent report prepared for the European Commission found that:

> "the decline of European competitiveness in pharmaceuticals is linked to the persistence of a fragmented market and, at the same time, to major 'non-market' and bureaucratic failures in public intervention and price regulation... [Governments should] converge on a higher reliance on innovative management methods and on competitive mechanisms, moving away from schemes excessively based on administrative decisions and bureaucratic structures/rules in the regulation of the market." (Gambardella 2001)

Government controls on pharmaceuticals also inhibit research on new uses for current drugs. Fixed prices based on a government-calculated "efficacy" of an existing drug would necessarily fail to capture newly-identified benefits. Such drugs as statins for treating high cholesterol and tissue plasminogen activator for treating stroke found some of their most valuable uses through major clinical trials after the drugs had already been approved for other purposes. (Calfee 2000)

Finally, countries that have relied on centralized approaches to controlling drug costs have generally not adopted U.S.-led innovations in "disease management" and "case management" approaches to reduce drug costs. These programs provide assistance to the many physicians who may be involved in the care of a patient with chronic illnesses or multiple illnesses, to ensure that the patient is receiving the most effective treatments for their conditions. For example, the Evercare program is a specialized health plan for frail elderly patients and others with multiple disabilities. These patients generally reside in nursing homes, or have substantial functional impairments that necessitate nursing home levels of care. Because they usually have multiple chronic illnesses, managing their prescription drug needs effectively can be complex. Often, individual physicians do not even have a complete understanding of all the medications that have been prescribed for their patients by various specialists. The Evercare program has specialized nurse practitioners who help the many medical professionals involved in the care of a frail elderly patient coordinate that care effectively, and who help the patient and their family gain better control of the patient's health needs. As a result, most patients in the Evercare program take up to eight prescriptions, whereas a typical nursing home resident takes 15 medications. Moreover, the program maintains a 95 percent satisfaction rate with families. Similar disease management programs that have been implemented by private insurance plans in Medicare help patients with diabetes, high blood pressure, heart failure, and other chronic illnesses reduce their medication needs and their medical complications.

EXAMPLES OF MEDICAL INNOVATIONS THAT HAVE IMPROVED THE QUALITY OF LIFE FOR AMERICAN SENIORS

Many seniors suffer from chronic diseases that have the potential to significantly interfere with their independence and well-being. In the past, as a result of these chronic conditions, many seniors became disabled and were forced to limit their activities. Advances in medical science and new pharmaceutical products have significantly improved the quality of life for seniors in this country, enabling many to live longer, more active, and independent lives. Medical conditions in which recent advances in pharmacotherapeutics have had a dramatic impact on the course of disease and, hence, quality of individuals' lives include cancer, osteoporosis, asthma, arthritis, high cholesterol, heart attacks, strokes, depression, Alzheimer's disease, type 2 diabetes, and migraine headaches.

However, due to government controls on access to drugs in other countries, patients who need new therapies often have to wait longer for them or may never have access to them at all. For example, in Western Europe, it took an average of 643 days for the initial approval and subsequent recognition of a drug by all European Commission countries, whereas in the U.S. it took an average of 335 days. (Davidson 2001) In Canada, approval of Rituxan®, a new treatment for non-Hodgkins lymphoma, took two more years after the drug was approved in the U.S. in 1998. (Evenson 2000) Moreover, in Canada, where patients often experience delays in treatment under the government health system, researchers attempting to quantify the cost of this waiting time for cardiac patients have estimated it to amount to $1,100 to $5,600 annually per patient. (Walker and Wilson 2001)

This section highlights recent pharmaceutical breakthroughs in the treatment of chronic diseases that are improving the life and longevity of American seniors, as well as exciting new drugs that are in the research pipeline. In addition, specific examples of reduced access to new drugs in countries with some form of government controls are discussed.

Cancer

- More than 550,000 Americans will die from cancer this year. (American Cancer Society 2002)

- The National Cancer Institute estimates that approximately 8.9 million Americans alive today have a history of cancer.

- If the current incidence pattern continues, cancer diagnoses will double from 1.3 million people in 2000 to 2.6 million people in 2050. Moreover, during this period, the number of cancer patients aged 85 and older is expected to increase four-fold.

- Cancer is one of the most expensive diseases to treat. In 2001, total costs for cancer were reported to be in excess of $156 billion, with medical expenditures accounting for approximately $56 billion. (American Cancer Society 2002)

- Recent advances in biotechnology have yielded some promising new approaches to cancer treatment.

Percentage of U.S. Adults who have ever had Cancer, by Age

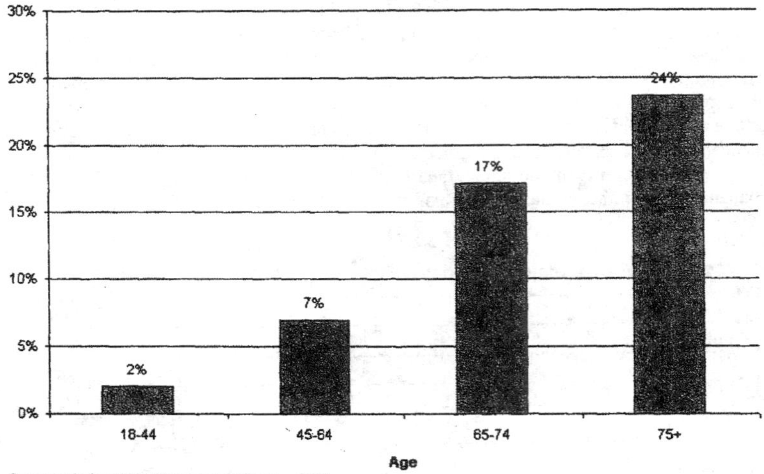

Source: National Health Interview Survey, 2000

Cancer is the second most common cause of death in the United States. Lung, colorectal, prostate, and breast cancer are the most common types of cancer. Although there has been an overall decline in U.S. cancer death rates, the cancer burden is expected to rise as the population ages. (NIH, National Cancer Institute 2002)

Lifetime Probability of Breast Cancer in Women in the United States

From age 30 to age 40	1 out of 257
From age 40 to age 50	1 out of 67
From age 50 to age 60	1 out of 36
From age 60 to age 70	1 out of 28
From age 70 to age 80	1 out of 24
Ever	1 out of 8

Source: National Cancer Institute Surveillance, Epidemiology, and End Results Program, 1995-1997

Treatment of Cancer

Treatment for cancer depends on the type of cancer; the size, location, and stage of disease; and the person's general health. Drugs and biologics play an important role in the treatment of cancer. Attempts to decipher the human genome have launched an exciting new era in biomedical research with tremendous potential for cancer treatment. New drugs are now being designed to target specific molecular features characteristic of cancer cells, including genetic mutations, epigenetic factors causing changes in gene expression, structural changes in the proteins that are products of mutated genes, and derangements in signal transduction pathways. In essence, any specific difference in the molecular composition of tumor cells can become the basis for "targeted" therapy. In the future, the treatment for each patient's cancer will be individualized based on the unique repertoire of molecular targets expressed by their particular tumor.

Percentage of U.S. Males who have Ever had Prostate Cancer, by Age

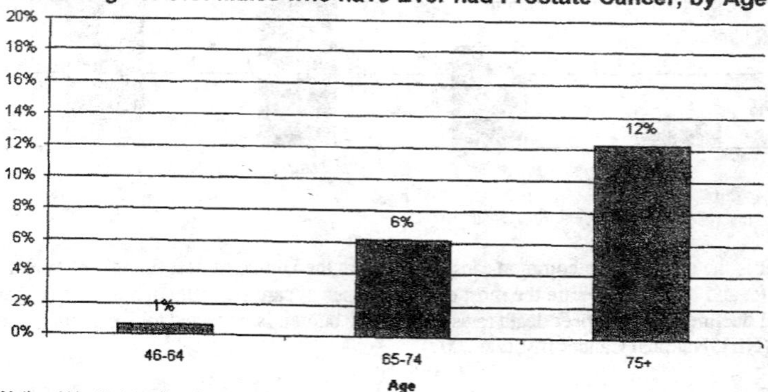

Source: National Health Interview Survey, 2000

Conventional anticancer drugs have tended to be non-selective, attacking both cancerous and healthy cells. Consequently, cancer chemotherapy is often accompanied by a variety of devastating short- or long-term side effects. Moreover, individual patient responses to conventional agents are highly variable, even in cases where specific cancers appear to be histologically identical. Molecularly targeted therapies based on recent progress in genomics and proteomics, however, hold out the promise of being far more selective, thereby drastically reducing the incidence of side effects in patients undergoing cancer treatment. (Livingston 2001)

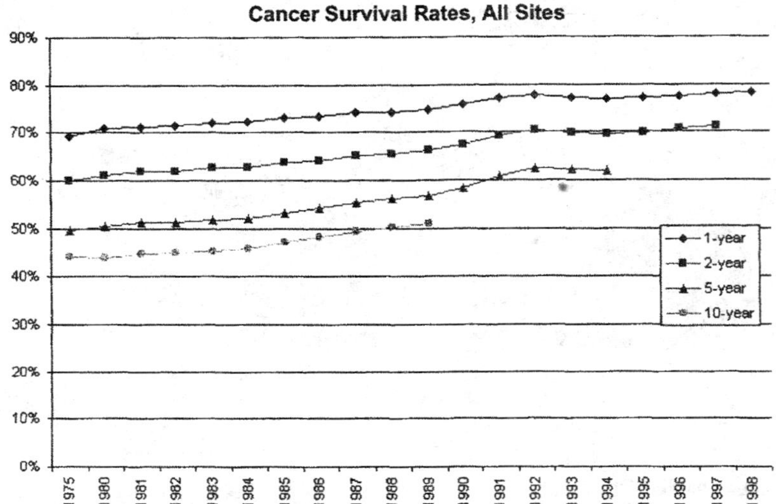

Note: The year is the year of diagnosis or death.
Source: Surveillance, Epidemiology, and End Results Cancer Statistics Review 1973-1999; National Cancer Institute, 2002.

For example, the recently FDA-approved drug, Gleevec, which is used to treat chronic myeloid leukemia (CML), is one of the first agents using this new approach that targets abnormal proteins fundamental to the cancer. (Wall Street Journal May 16, 2002) Unlike most current cancer therapies that kill both normal and cancer cells leading to unwanted side-effects, Gleevec and other drugs in this class are designed to zero in on specific cancer-causing molecules, eliminating cancer cells while avoiding serious damage to other, non-cancerous cells. Early studies of this drug have shown that in patients with chronic myelocytic leukemia, white blood-cell counts are restored to normal levels.

Although Gleevec® is available in the U.S., other countries have restricted its use. For example, the preliminary review of Gleevec in the UK by officials at the government-sponsored National Institute for Clinical Excellence recommended that the drug only be used in patients who had already gone into the "accelerated phase" of their disease. (Hawkes 2002) In the U.S., Gleevec is indicated for treatment of patients with CML in blast crisis, the accelerated phase or in chronic phase after failure of interferon-alpha therapy.

Gleevec: HOW IT WORKS

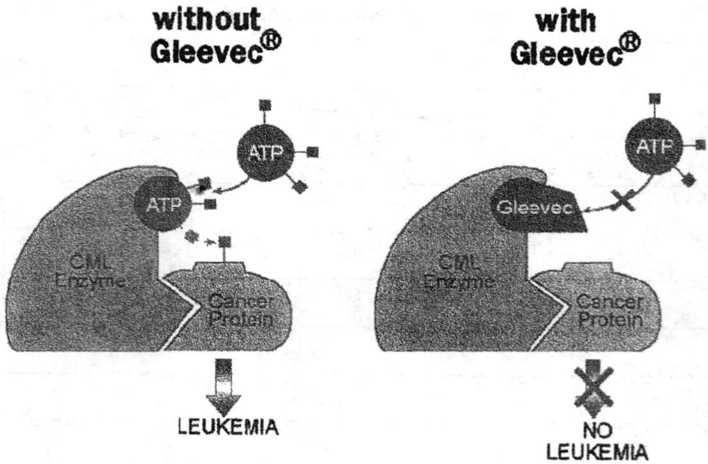

<u>Drugs in the pipeline for cancer</u>

- Drugs and biologics that target specific molecules or proteins on cancer cells are being developed. (NIH 2002, Livingston 2001)

- Vaccines against certain types of cancer are also being investigated. (NIH 2002, Livingston 2001)

- Drugs that prevent blood vessel growth in tumors are also being tested. (NIH 2002, Margolin 2001)

At present, many new compounds, some of which have novel mechanisms of action, are in development. In 2002, 402 drugs or biologics are in clinical trials for treatment of various forms of cancer. (PhRMA 2002)

Several new approaches to treat cancer are being investigated. Much research is underway to develop drugs and biologics that attack certain molecular targets on cancer cells, causing selective cell death. (NIH 2002, Livingston 2001) By specifically targeting cancer cells, damage to normal cells will be minimized, thus reducing the morbidity of chemotherapy.

Scientists are also studying different compounds that work with the body's immune system to kill cancer cells. One clinical trial is evaluating the ability of an antibody to kill lymphoma cells. In other trials, agents that manipulate different parts of the immune response to kill tumor cells are under investigation. (NIH 2002)

Tumor growth is dependent on the generation of new blood vessels to maintain blood supply to cancer cells. This new blood vessel formation is called angiogenesis. Anti-angiogenic drugs that block a tumor's ability to grow new blood vessels are in clinical trials. (NIH 2002, Margolin 2001) Finally, there is interest in developing vaccines for different types of tumors, such as colon cancer and melanoma. (NIH 2002, Livingston 2001, American Cancer Society 2002)

Osteoporosis

- In the U.S. today, 10 million individuals already have osteoporosis and 18 million more have low bone mass, placing them at increased risk for the disease.

- Osteoporosis is responsible for more than 1.5 million fractures annually, including 300,000 hip fractures, and approximately 700,000 vertebral fractures, 250,000 wrist fractures, and more than 300,000 fractures at other sites.

- It is estimated that approximately one out of two women and one out of eight men over 50 will sustain one or more osteoporosis-related fractures of the spine, hip, or wrist during their remaining lifetimes.

- Effective treatments are available to prevent osteoporosis and reduce the risk of debilitating fractures.

Percentage of Females Age 65 or Older who have Osteoporosis, by Race/Ethnicity

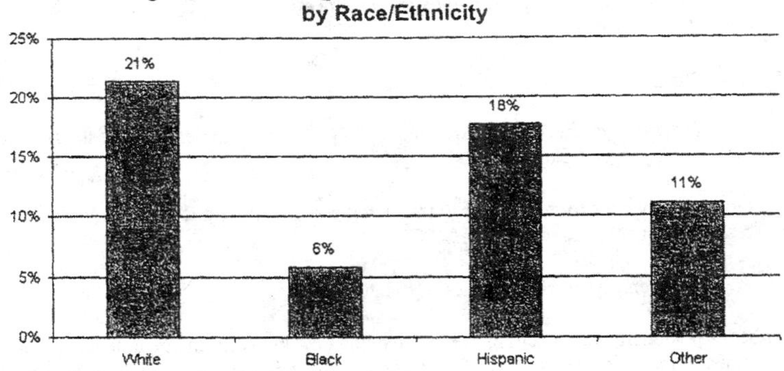

Source: 1998 Medicare Current Beneficiary Survey

Osteoporosis is a major public health threat for 28 million Americans, 80 percent of whom are women. (NIH 2002) Osteoporosis is characterized by low bone mass that leads to an increased risk of fracture, most frequently of the spine, hip, or wrist. Osteoporosis occurs in both men and women but is most common in post-menopausal women. Osteoporotic hip fractures, in particular, are associated with substantial morbidity, disability, and mortality. Moreover, only one-third of hip fracture patients will return to pre-fracture independence. (U. of Washington 2002) Estimated national direct expenditures (hospitals and nursing homes) for osteoporosis and related fractures are about $14 billion a year.

Treatment of osteoporosis

Osteoporosis is largely a preventable and treatable disease. Comprehensive treatment programs that focus on proper nutrition, exercise, medication, and prevention of falls, can slow or stop bone loss, increase bone density, and reduce fracture risk. (NIH 2002) First introduced in the mid-1990s, bisphosphonates, which inhibit bone reabsorption, represent one recent category of pharmaceuticals that effectively treat osteoporosis. (National Osteoporosis Foundation 2002) Alendronate and risedronate are in this category of drugs. In one study, risedronate significantly reduced the risk of hip fractures in elderly women with a confirmed diagnosis of osteoporosis. (McClung 2001)

Although treatment with these agents significantly reduces the risk of developing osteoporosis and subsequent fractures, some countries restrict reimbursement for these drugs to relatively narrow categories of patients. For example, in New Zealand, only specialists can initiate therapy with Fosamax®, a bisphosphonate, and then only after the patient has already suffered one previous, significant osteoporotic fracture (radiologically demonstrated) and has a substantially low bone mass density. (Merck & Co. 2002) Australia, Italy, Belgium, and France have similar restrictions on reimbursement for Fosamax®. In Ontario, Canada, Fosamax® is only reimbursed for treatment of osteoporosis in post-menopausal women who have failed to respond to etidronate (which is not even a mainstream treatment in the U.S. for osteoporosis), as evidenced by continued loss of bone mineral density after two years of treatment, a new fracture after one year of etidronate therapy, or intractable side effects or allergic reaction from etidronate. (Merck & Co. 2002)

Drugs in the pipeline for osteoporosis

- Selective Estrogen Receptor Modulators (SERMS)- mimic the effects of estrogen and prevent bone loss. (Ettinger 1999)

- Novel approaches for new drugs to treat osteoporosis target different elements in bone reabsorption and formation. (NIH 2002)

- Phytoestrogens are in clinical trials. (NIH 2002)

A number of potentially very exciting agents are being developed for the treatment of osteoporosis. Some of these may have fewer side effects and, therefore, may be better tolerated by patients. Fifteen drugs were in clinical trials for osteoporosis in 2002. (PhRMA 2002)

These agents can be divided into two categories: those that prevent bone reabsorption and those that promote new bone formation. Different elements involved in maintaining healthy bone are targeted by these new compounds, including factors involved in bone cell function and regulation, cell membrane receptors and attachment proteins, and cellular enzymes and nuclear transcription factors. (Tobias 2002; Boskey 2001)

For example, a new class of drugs called Selective Estrogen Receptor Modulators (SERMS) prevents bone loss and reduces the risk of fractures, by mimicking the effects of estrogen in some parts of the body. (National Osteoporosis Foundation 2002) Raloxifene is one of the first SERMS available.

Both Ontario and Quebec, Canada, limit coverage for raloxifene. Ontario's formulary approves raloxifene treatment only for postmenopausal women who have failed to respond to etidronate (as evidenced by continued loss of bone mineral density after two years of therapy), have experienced a new osteoporosis related fracture after one year of etidronate treatment, or have experienced intractable side effects or allergy with etidronate which precludes continuation of therapy. (Ontario Ministry of Health and Long Term Care 2002) In Quebec, raloxifene treatment is not listed as an approved therapy on Quebec's formulary. (Quebec Prescription Drug Insurance Plan 2002)

In the near future, other agents may be available to treat osteoporosis. Phytoestrogens, substances derived from soy, are being tested to determine if they can reduce bone loss in older women. Many women are electing to try "natural" estrogens because these products are readily available and seem to work as selective estrogen receptor modulators. That is, they stimulate estrogen receptors on bone and slow bone breakdown, but have tissue selectivity that maximizes benefits and depresses harmful side effects. (NIH 2002)

Nitroglycerine is a drug used to treat angina pectoris (a recurring pain or discomfort in the chest that happens when some part of the heart does not receive enough blood) that has been shown in pilot studies to reduce bone loss in women who have had their ovaries removed. (NIH 2002) Nitroglycerin releases a substance (nitric oxide) that is a powerful mediator of hormone action. It is being tested in postmenopausal women, but if found to be effective could work equally well in men.

Asthma

- In 1999, 26.7 million people in the U.S. reported that they had been diagnosed with asthma sometime in their lives, and 10.5 million had experienced an asthma attack or episode in the previous 12 months. (CDC 2002)

- 7.6 percent of seniors report having asthma. (CDC 2002)

- In 1999, there were 11 million visits for asthma to private physician offices and outpatient departments, 2 million visits to the emergency department, and about one-half million hospitalizations. (CDC 2002)

- In 1999, 4,657 people died from asthma, at a rate of 1.7 per 100,000 population. (CDC 2002)

Asthma is a chronic respiratory disease involving episodes or attacks of small airway narrowing from inflammation and hyper-responsiveness to asthma "triggers." Triggers may include allergens, infections, exercise, abrupt changes in the weather, and exposure to environmental irritants such as cigarette smoke. Asthma attacks can vary from mild to life threatening, and involve shortness of breath, coughing, wheezing, chest pain or tightness, or a combination of these symptoms. Asthma has become more common over the past two decades, and it remains a key public health problem in the United States. (MMWR 2002)

Treatment of asthma

In addition to avoiding triggers, treatment of asthma usually consists of some combination of bronchodilators and anti-inflammatory agents. Bronchodilators work to relax the muscles in airway walls, opening breathing passages. Anti-inflammatory drugs work to reduce swelling, inflammation, and mucous in airways thereby relieving some of the obstruction to airflow. Corticosteroids are one common class of anti-inflammatory drugs used in treating asthma. Although effective, long-term treatment with corticosteroids, particularly when taken by pill, may have significant side effects, such as bone mineral loss, weight gain, and stomach irritation.. A few nonsteroidal pharmaceuticals to reduce airway inflammation are currently available. These agents do not have the side effects that corticosteroids may produce. (Gawchik 2000)

Recently introduced leukotriene antagonists represent the first truly new approach in treating asthma in the past 30 years. Montelukast, a leukotriene receptor antagonist, is the first in this class that targets a specific receptor for a substance that is involved in the inflammatory response in the airways. Since this drug inhibits the inflammatory response, it is indicated for prophylaxis to reduce asthma attacks. Use of montelukast may eliminate or decrease the need for chronic use of inhaled corticosteroids, which can have significant side effects and which are difficult for some patients to use effectively. (Lipworth 1999)

Montelukast (Singulair®) is approved in the U.S. for the prophylaxis and chronic treatment of asthma. New Zealand, Australia, Belgium and Finland do not currently provide coverage for this medication. In addition, many provinces in Canada restrict coverage of montelukast only to patients who are not able to control their asthma symptoms with inhaled corticosteroids. (Quebec Prescription Drug Insurance Plan)

Drugs in the pipeline for asthma

- Novel agents for the treatment of asthma that target different parts of the inflammatory cascade are in clinical development. These include compounds that target cells, antibodies, cell receptors, mediators, and cell signaling substances. (Hansel 2001)

- Preliminary studies of selective enzyme inhibitors have shown promise. (Szelenyi 2002)

- New glucocorticoids with less severe side effects are being developed. (Szelenyi 2002)

Numerous agents that attack different parts of the inflammatory response seen in asthma are in clinical development. (Crystal 2001, PhRMA 2002) By disrupting the inflammatory cascade and reducing airway inflammation, asthma may be better controlled and acute attacks prevented. These compounds target specific cells, antibodies, inflammatory mediators, cell surface proteins, and cell signaling substances that are involved in producing an acute asthma attack. (Hansel 2001) In addition, there are efforts to produce new corticosteroids that have significantly fewer side effects. (Szelenyi 2002) PhRMA reports that twenty-seven medications are currently in clinical trials for the treatment of asthma. (PhRMA 2002)

Arthritis

Percentage of Adults with Arthritic Symptoms by Age, 2000

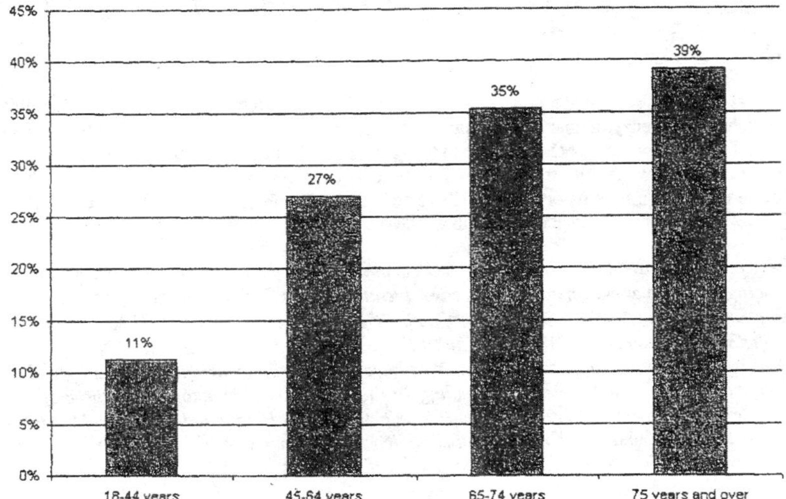

Note: Respondents were asked if they had experienced pain, aching, stiffness, or swelling in or around a joint that was present most days for at least one month.
Source: National Health Interview Survey, 2000

- Arthritis is the leading cause of disability in the United States.
- In this country, about one of every six people (43 million) has arthritis, and the disease limits the daily activities of seven million people.
- Approximately 21 million Americans suffer from osteoarthritis; 75% of them are women. By 2020, if current rates continue, 60 million people will have the disease, and 11 million will have activity limitations.

- Forty percent of people with arthritis are age 65 or older.

- Pharmaceutical agents are available to control the disabling symptoms, especially pain, of arthritis.

Arthritis is not a single disease but rather it is an umbrella term for a group of more than 100 conditions that involve the joints and surrounding tissues, including osteoarthritis, rheumatoid arthritis, gout, and bursitis. (CDC 1999) All of these conditions can decrease quality of life, causing pain and limiting people's ability to engage in the activities of daily living. Besides the physical toll, arthritis costs the U.S. nearly $65 billion annually. (CDC 2002) Although cost-effective interventions are available to reduce the burden of arthritis, they are currently underutilized.

New treatments for arthritis

COX-2 inhibitors represent a newer class of medications used to treat arthritis. COX-2 inhibitors interfere with an enzyme that causes pain and swelling. Moreover, these drugs do not inhibit the COX-1 enzyme, which may help maintain the normal stomach lining. Thus, COX-2 inhibitors are reported to have less gastrointestinal side effects than older drugs, such as aspirin or other nonsteroidal anti-inflammatory agents. (Silverstein 2000; Bombardier 2000) Included in the COX-2 class are rofecoxib and celecoxib.

Despite the wide availability and use of COX-2 inhibitors in the U.S., some countries restrict coverage of these agents or provide no coverage at all. New Zealand has not approved reimbursement for Celebrex® or Vioxx®, both COX-2 inhibitors. (PHARMAC 2002) In Ontario, Canada, reimbursement for Vioxx® is limited to patients with osteoarthritis who have failed prior treatment with acetaminophen, and who have a history of documented, clinically significant ulcer or gastrointestinal bleeding, or failure or intolerance to at least three other non-steroidal anti-inflammatory agents. (Ontario Ministry of Health and Long Term Care 2002) In addition, reimbursement for this drug is limited to a maximum daily dose of 25 mg, which is not always sufficient to provide effective control of symptoms.

Recent advances in biotechnology have produced novel approaches to treat arthritis. Biologic response modifiers are genetically engineered substances used to reduce the signs and symptoms of rheumatoid arthritis. (Paget 2002) Drugs in this class include etanercept, anakinra, and infliximab. Etanercept, the first in this new class of drugs, acts by inhibiting tumor necrosis factor (TNF), one of the proteins that plays an important role in the cascade of reactions that causes the inflammatory process of rheumatoid arthritis, resulting in significant reduction in inflammatory activity. Infliximab, a monoclonal antibody, also inhibits TNF. Anakinra is a recombinant IL-1 receptor antagonist that also modifies the inflammatory response.

Both etanercept and infliximab are approved by the FDA, but have limited availablity in other countries. These drugs are not covered in New Zealand, or Ontario, Canada and their use in the UK is restricted to patients who have failed arthritis treatments with other medications. (National Institute for Clinical Excellence 2002; PHARMAC 2002; Ontario Ministry of Health and Long Term Care 2001)

Drugs in the pipeline for arthritis

- Additional inflammatory response modulators to reduce the inflammation of arthritis are being studied. (Koopman 2001)

- A vaccine for rheumatoid arthritis which would prevent the autoimmune response is in development. (PhRMA 2002)

Pharmaceutical approaches that modify the inflammatory or immune response are likely candidates for new drugs to treat arthritis. (Koopman 2001) In 2002, eight new drugs for osteoarthritis were undergoing clinical trials. (PhRMA 2002) In addition, clinical trials for 22 new medications for rheumatoid arthritis, including a vaccine to prevent the autoimmune process that causes the disease, were in progress in 2002. (PhRMA 2002)

High Cholesterol

- Approximately 25 percent of the adult population in the U.S. has elevated blood cholesterol levels. (NIH 2002)

- A high blood cholesterol level is a major risk factor for heart disease and stroke.

- Drug therapy can effectively lower blood cholesterol.

Cholesterol is a soft, waxy substance produced by the body and found in foods of animal origin. It is present in the blood stream and all body cells. Since cholesterol cannot dissolve in the blood, it is transported to and from the cells by two main lipoprotein carriers: LDL (low-density lipoprotein) and HDL (high-density lipoprotein). A high blood LDL-cholesterol is one of the major risk factors for coronary artery disease, which leads to heart attacks. In contrast, a high level of HDL-cholesterol tends to protect against heart disease. The higher one's blood LDL-cholesterol level, the greater the risk for developing heart disease or having a heart attack.

Treatment of high cholesterol

Since an elevated LDL-cholesterol significantly increases the risk of heart disease, treatment is directed at lowering blood levels. Statins represent a new category of LDL-cholesterol lowering drugs. There are currently five statin drugs on the market: lovastatin, pravastatin, simvastatin, fluvastatin, and atorvastatin. Research has demonstrated that the use of statins results in large reductions of total and LDL-cholesterol, which decreases heart attacks and heart disease deaths. (NIH 2002) Studies using statins have reported 20 to 60 percent lower LDL-cholesterol levels in patients taking these drugs. (American Heart Association 2002) Current research findings are pointing to other possible benefits of statins, indicating that they may be helpful in preventing and treating a variety of conditions, including cancer, strokes, Alzheimer's, adult-onset diabetes, deep vein thrombosis, and organ rejection in transplantation. (Bellosta 2000)

Percentage of 65-74 Year-olds with High Serum Cholesterol

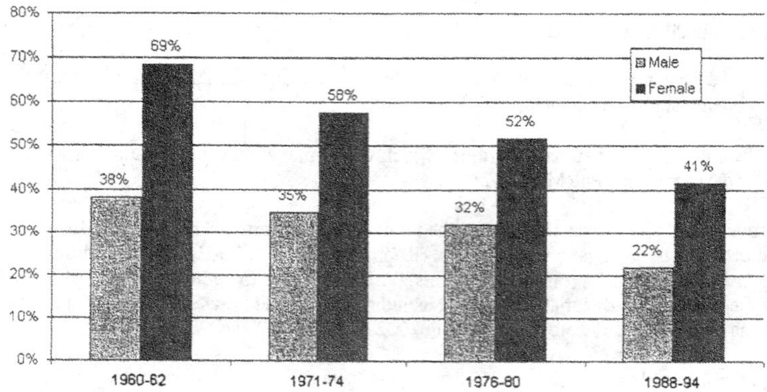

Source: National Health and Nutrition Examination Survey

Despite the wide use of statins to lower blood cholesterol in the United States, some countries limit access to this class of drugs. For example, Simvastatin (Zocor®) is a statin that is used to lower blood cholesterol. In Australia, reimbursement for Zocor® is restricted to patients who fail six weeks of dietary therapy. In New Zealand, only three of the five FDA-approved statins are covered by the government's health plan. (PHARMAC 2002)

<u>Drugs in the pipeline for high cholesterol</u>

- Drugs designed to interfere with intestinal reabsorption of cholesterol are being investigated. (NIH 2002, Leitersdorf 2002)

- Drugs that inhibit the cholesteryl ester transfer protein (CETP inhibitors) are in development. These drugs would work synergistically with statins to lower blood cholesterol. (NIH 2002, de Grooth 2002)

- Vaccines that prevent the conversion of HDL to LDL cholesterol are under study. (PhRMA 2002)

New pharmaceutical approaches to elevated blood cholesterol are in development. Research is underway on an investigational drug (a cholesterol absorption inhibitor) that may provide additional reductions in LDL cholesterol when taken along with some statins. (Leitersdorf 2002) In addition, PhRMA reports that there is an effort to develop a vaccine that will lower blood cholesterol by preventing the conversion of HDL-cholesterol to LDL-cholesterol. (PhRMA 2002)

Cardiovascular Disease—Heart Disease and Stroke

- About 950,000 Americans die of cardiovascular disease each year, which amounts to one death every 33 seconds.

- Eighty-three percent of people who die from coronary heart disease are age 65 or older. (American Heart Association 2001)

- Seventy-two percent of people who suffer a stroke in a given year are 65 or older. (American Heart Association 2001)

- New therapies for heart attacks and strokes have reduced the morbidity and improved the mortality in patients experiencing these events.

The Percentage of Persons 65 Years of Age and Over who have had a stroke

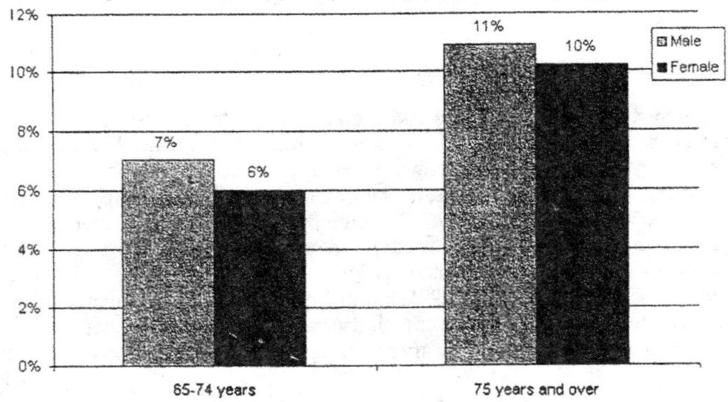

Source: National Health Interview Survey, 2000

Heart disease and stroke—the principal components of cardiovascular diseases—are the first and third leading causes of death in the United States, accounting for more than 40% of deaths. (CDC 2002) However, a consideration of deaths alone understates the burden of cardiovascular disease. About 61 million Americans (almost one fourth of the population) live with this disease. Stroke alone accounts for disability among more than 4 million Americans. Almost 6 million hospitalizations each year are due to cardiovascular disease.

Predictably, strokes and heart attacks have a higher incidence in seniors. High blood pressure and diabetes are chronic conditions that predispose individuals to develop cardiovascular disease. Both diseases have a relatively high prevalence in seniors.

Percentage of Persons 65 Years of Age or Over with Coronary Heart Disease, 2000

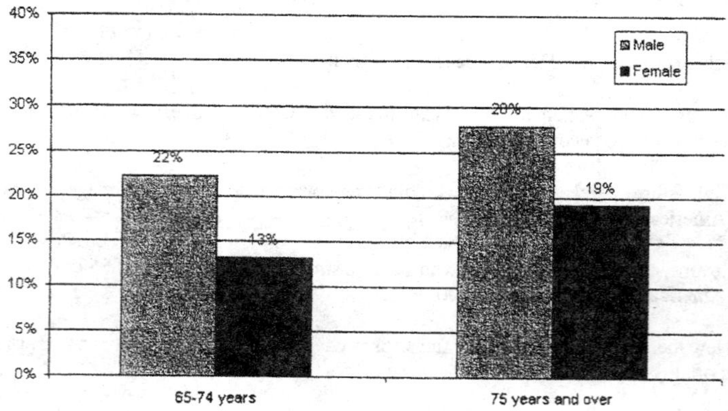

Note: Coronary heart disease includes coronary heart disease, angina, and heart attack.
Source: National Health Interview Survey

Newer treatments for cardiovascular disease

Recently developed treatment approaches for heart attacks and strokes have reduced the morbidity and improved the mortality in patients experiencing these events. For example, Tissue Plasminogen Activator (t-PA) is a thrombolytic agent, known as a "clot-busting" drug. It can dissolve blood clots, which cause most heart attacks and strokes. The FDA approved the use of t-PA for treatment of some strokes in 1996. The prompt use (within the first three hours) of t-PA following an ischemic stroke has been shown to halt damage and significantly improve recovery. In addition, prompt treatment of stroke victims with t-PA could result in substantial net cost savings to the health care system. (NIH 1995; Fagan 1998) These savings are based on the fact that t-PA-treated stroke patients, because of their decreased disability, leave the hospital sooner and require less rehabilitation and nursing after discharge than do patients who do not receive t-PA.

GP IIb/IIIa inhibitors are another example of newer pharmaceuticals that reduce the risk of atherosclerotic events (myocardial infarction and stroke) in patients with atherosclerosis documented by recent stroke, recent myocardial infarctions, or established peripheral arterial disease. (Sabatine 2000) These drugs inhibit platelet aggregation (platelet blockers), which is a factor in the initiation or evolution of acute cardiovascular or cerebrovascular events. GP IIb/IIIa inhibitors include clopidogrel, eptifibatide, and tirofiban.

In recent years, there have been significant advances in the treatment of chronic conditions, such as hypertension, that place patients at elevated risk for strokes and other cardiovascular diseases. For example, angiotensin II receptor antagonists—losartan (Cozaar®) and valsartan (Diovan®)—represent relatively new therapies for the treatment of hypertension, a primary risk factor for heart attacks and strokes. These drugs are readily available and widely used in the U.S. to treat high blood pressure, and are preferred by many patients and doctors because of their effectiveness and the absence of side effects in many patients. However, they are often not covered in other countries. For example, as a result of formulary restrictions in Ontario and other Canadian provinces, access to these drugs is restricted to patients who have proven that they cannot tolerate other high-blood pressure medications. (Ontario Ministry of Health and Long Term Care 2001) In Australia, although Cozaar® treatment was reimbursed approximately six years ago, the government instituted further cost controls, and as a result the drug is no longer sold in Australia. (Merck & Co. 2002) In New Zealand, only specialists (cardiologists) can initiate therapy with Cozaar®, and then only after the patient has developed congestive heart failure and has failed treatment attempts with at least two kinds of angiotensin converting enzyme (ACE) inhibitors. Diovan® is not approved for coverage in New Zealand. (PHARMAC 2002)

The Percentage of Persons 65 Years of Age and Over with Hypertension, 2000

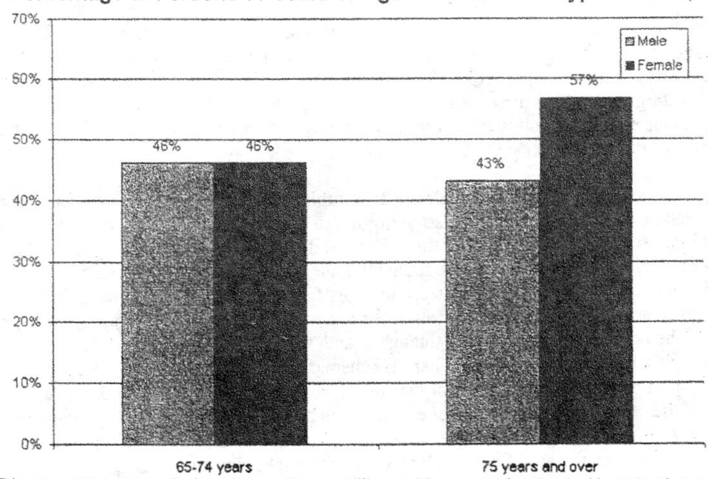

Note: This represents persons who have been told on two different visits or more that they had hypertension or high blood pressure.
Source: National Health Interview Survey, 2000

Drugs in the pipeline to treat cardiovascular disease

- Research is underway on a clot-dissolving drug made from the venom of a pit viper snake. (Sherman 2000)

- Pharmaceutical approaches to limit brain damage and to aid recovery of stroke victims represent new approaches to treatment. (NIH 2002)

- A drug that lowers the heart's need for oxygen may protect the heart muscle from damage during a heart attack. (NIH 2002, PhRMA 2002)

- Angiogenic therapies to revascularize the heart muscle are being investigated. (NIH 2002)

Advances in medical science have yielded new approaches to the treatment of cardiovascular disease. (Lefkowitz 2001) PhRMA reports that 122 new medicines are in development for cardiovascular diseases in 2002. (PhRMA 2002) Some of these new agents are directed at chronic medical conditions that are risk factors for the development of heart disease, such as high blood pressure or high cholesterol. Other compounds are new treatments for complications of heart disease including congestive heart failure and arrhythmias. For example, B-natriuretic peptide (BNP) is a small protein produced by the heart muscle that improves cardiac function. A recombinant form of BNP was recently approved by the FDA for the treatment of decompensated congestive heart failure. (NIH 2002) Other potential uses of BNP are currently being investigated.

Two broad, complementary strategies are under development, which aim to reduce morbidity from a stroke. One is to restore blood flow to the brain as quickly as possible and another is to limit the damage incurred by a stroke. Similar to t-PA, the venom of a pit viper snake is a clot-dissolving drug. While this drug has not been approved yet, early findings suggest that it helps stroke patients regain their physical and mental abilities, with many patients experiencing full recovery. (Sherman 2000)

The NIH reports that several compounds that may limit brain damage in stroke victims are now being tested in animal models. Scientists are trying to develop "neuroprotective drugs" that prevent strokes from damaging brain cells. Efforts to develop neuroprotective drugs build on very substantial research efforts that are unraveling the complex cascade of harmful events that occur in the brain in the seconds, minutes, and hours following a stroke. Each step in the cascade presents a potential target for drug intervention. Excitotoxicity occurs from excessive release of the normal neurotransmitter glutamate, and, when challenged by stroke, brain cells produce highly reactive and potentially harmful chemicals called "free radicals." Research is developing drugs that intervene at various stages of excitotoxicity, free radical damage, and other aspects of the stroke-induced cascade of events in the brain. For example, anti-oxidants to prevent free-radical damage are being evaluated. As another example, amapakines are drugs that act by modulating a subclass of nerve cell receptors for a specific neurotransmitter. Excessive release of this neurotransmitter can cause damage in stroke victims. Testing is being conducted to determine if amapakines can prevent brain damage from stroke or help improve learning and memory following stroke. (NIH 2002)

Finally, scientists have been encouraged by recent findings that the adult human brain has a surprising capacity to adapt following disease or injury, even to the extent of making new nerve cells. As a result, researchers are trying to develop drug interventions that enhance the brain's capacity to repair itself.

Benign Prostatic Hyperplasia (BPH)

- More than half of men in their sixties and 90 percent in their seventies have some symptoms of BPH.

- In the United States, 375,000 hospital stays each year involve a diagnosis of BPH.

As a man ages, it is common for the prostate gland to become enlarged. This condition is called benign prostatic hyperplasia (BPH). Although BPH rarely causes symptoms before the age of 40, an increasing percentage of men will become symptomatic as they get older. Symptoms of BPH stem from obstruction of the urethra and gradual loss of bladder function, which results in incomplete emptying of the bladder. Common complaints of BPH include urinary urgency and frequency, and multiple instances of nocturnal urination.

<u>Treatment of BPH</u>

Four drugs are approved by the FDA to treat BPH. One drug, finasteride (Proscar®), inhibits production of a hormone which is involved with prostate enlargement. *Although widely used in the United States, finasteride (Proscar®) is not covered in New Zealand or Ontario, Canada. (Ontario Ministry of Health and Long Term Care 2001; PHARMAC 2002)*

Three newer drugs, alpha-1 blockers (alpha-1 adrenoceptor antagonists), act to relax the smooth muscle of the prostate and bladder neck to improve urine flow and to reduce bladder outlet obstruction. Using an alpha-1 blocker along with finasteride is more effective than either drug alone to relieve the symptoms and prevent BPH progression. (NIH, NIDDK 2002) The two-drug regimen reduced the risk of BPH progression by 67 percent, compared to 39 percent for an alpha blocker alone or 34 percent for finasteride alone.

<u>Drugs in the pipeline for BPH</u>

- Studies to evaluate phytotherapeutic agents to treat BPH are under way. (NIH 2002, Andersson 2002) [NIDDK and the National Center for Complementary and Alternative Medicine (NCCAM) currently fund a small, single-center pilot project using saw palmetto for BPH, and plan to fund a large, multi-center clinical trial using *Serenoa repens* (saw palmetto) and *Pygeum africanum* in men with BPH, beginning on about September 30, 2002.]

- Endothelin and muscarinic receptor antagonists are being evaluated for the treatment of BPH. (Andersson 2002)

- Subtypes of alpha-1 blockers are being investigated. (Andersson 2002)

CNS neuronal uptake of serotonin. SSRIs include fluoxetine, paroxetine, citalopram, and sertraline.

Other recently introduced anti-depressants include the serotonin and noradrenaline reuptake inhibitors (SNRIs), venlafaxine and milnacipran. These drugs have a mechanism of action that is similar to the tricyclic antidepressants. Another new drug is reboxetine, a selective noradrenaline reuptake inhibitor. All these newer antidepressants may be better tolerated by patients suffering from depression.

Available in the United States since the 1980s, the first SSRI treatment was not available in Japan until 1999. Perhaps related to the relative unavailability of depression medication, Japan has the highest number of psychiatric inpatient beds in the world, in both absolute and relative terms. (Tajima 2001)

Drugs in the pipeline for depression

- Nicotinic-receptor stimulators to enhance cognitive function are being tested for the treatment of depression. (NIH 2002)
- New inhibitors of neurotransmitter uptake are being studied. (NIH 2002)
- Two compounds that act as antagonists for the glucocorticoid receptor (GR) are currently being studied in patients with severe major depression. (NIH 2002)
- Antagonists of substance P and corticotropin-releasing factor receptors are in clinical trials for the treatment of depression. (NIH 2002, Pacher 2001)
- Agonists and antagonists of different serotonin (5-HT) receptor subtypes are being investigated as potential antidepressants. (NIH 2002, Pacher 2001)

According to the Pharmaceutical Research and Manufacturers of America (PhRMA), 26 drugs for depression were in clinical trials in 2002. As medical science progresses, more effective and better tolerated treatments for depression will become available. Two principal strategies guide medication development efforts for depression. First, there are efforts to refine and reformulate existing medications known to work on "classic" neurotransmitter systems as a means of bringing more effective treatments to an expanded and more diverse population of persons with depression. Second, researchers are attempting to develop fundamentally new compounds that target novel brain mechanisms suggested by cutting edge research on the causes of depression.

Newer approaches to pharmaceutical treatment of depression target neuropeptide receptors and intracellular messenger systems. (Pacher 2001) Medications for depression currently under development include: corticotrophin releasing factor (CRF) receptor antagonists, substance P (neurokinin) receptor antagonists, and drugs that modulate glutamatergic transmission. (NIH 2002) Patients may tolerate these agents better than current drugs and, therefore, be more compliant with treatment regimens.

Abundant evidence suggests that increased production and/or release of CRF within the central nervous system occurs in patients with post-traumatic stress disorder and major depression. Preclinical studies show that CRF antagonists have anti-anxiety and antidepressant properties. Although CRF receptor antagonists appear promising as a novel class of antidepressants and anxiolytics, further study is needed into their clinical efficacy and safety.

Based on preclinical evidence suggesting anti-anxiety properties of inhibitors of the Substance P, selective compounds have been tested and found superior to placebo and equal to other antidepressants in treating depression. More evaluation of these agents is needed.

The neurotransmitter, glutamate, has been linked to anxiety and depression. Compounds that interfere with its action in the brain are among the candidate medications under development as potential antidepressants. (NIH 2002)

In addition to the approaches discussed, that have already led to the developing and testing of new types of antidepressants, rapid advances in neuroscience suggest medication development strategies that have yet to be undertaken. These include drugs that interact with second messenger systems, response elements and transcription factors, agents that enhance neuroprotective and neurogenic factors, and compounds that manipulate cytokine receptor activity.

Alzheimer's Disease

- An estimated 4 million Americans have Alzheimer's disease, a progressive, degenerative disorder. (CDC 1999)

- Approximately 10 percent of people older than 65 years and 47 percent of those older than 85 years have the disease.

- New therapies to reduce the morbidity and mortality of Alzheimer's disease are in development.

Symptoms of Alzheimer's disease may include memory loss, cognitive deficits in language, object recognition and executive functioning, and behavioral symptoms such as psychosis, agitation, depression, and wandering. The death rate for people with Alzheimer's disease is twice as great as the rate among those of the same age without the disease. Although less than three percent of the population has Alzheimer's disease at age 65, the prevalence doubles every five years thereafter. Because the risk of Alzheimer's disease increases with age, the prevalence of the disease is anticipated to increase as the U.S. population ages. This will incur a substantial economic and social burden. The estimated annual economic toll of health care expenses due to Alzheimer's patients and caregivers in the U.S. is $80 to $100 billion. (CDC 1999) This estimate includes both direct and indirect costs for medical and long-term care, home care, and loss of productivity for caregivers. Costs are especially high among patients with behavioral symptoms, who often require earlier or more frequent institutionalization.

Pharmaceutical treatment of Alzheimer's disease

Early Alzheimer's disease is marked by a deficiency of acetylcholine in critical areas of the brain which is believed to account for some of the clinical manifestations of mild to moderate dementia. Cholinesterase inhibitors act to raise the concentration of acetylcholine in the brain by slowing the degradation of acetylcholine. Newer drugs included in this category are donepezil, tacrine, galantamine, and rivastigmine. Treating persons suffering with Alzheimer's disease with these new drugs may help to maintain function and may ease the burden on caregivers for a limited period of time.

Donepezil (Aricept®) is not approved for coverage in Quebec, Canada or New Zealand. (Quebec Prescription Drug Insurance Plan 2002; PHARMAC 2002) Tacrine, an acetyl cholinesterase inhibitor available in the U.S., is currently not registered for use in New Zealand. (New Zealand Guidelines Group 2002)

Percentage of Older Adults who have Alzheimer's Disease, by Age

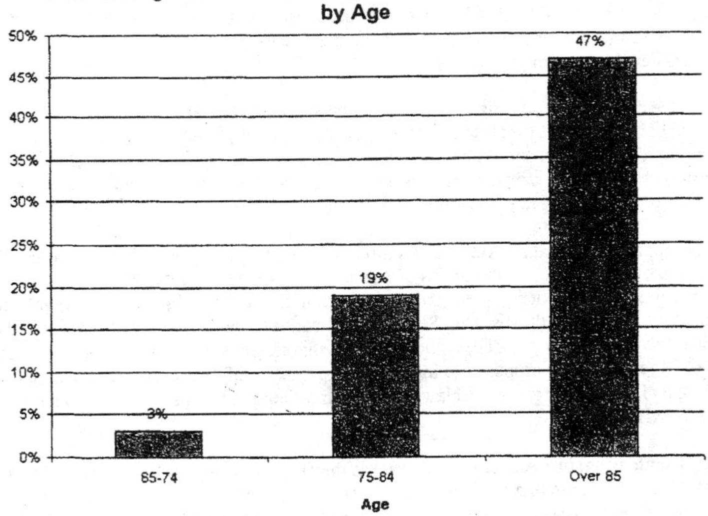

Source: D. Evans, et. al., JAMA, vol. 262, no. 18, 1989.

Drugs in the pipeline to treat Alzheimer's disease

Over 20 clinical trials of new drugs to treat Alzheimer's disease were underway in 2001 (PhRMA 2002) and a similar number were funded by the NIH. These include:

- A new approach under development for the treatment of Alzheimer's disease is to use drugs to limit the neurotoxicity mediated by microglia. (NIH 2002)

- Anti-oxidants and anti-inflammatory agents are being tested for effectiveness in treating Alzheimer's disease. (NIH 2002, Alzheimer's Research Forum 2002)

- A compound that activates neural growth factors in the brain is being tested. (Alzheimer's Association 2002)

- A drug that increases signaling between nerve cells is also under study. (NIH 2002, Alzheimer's Research Forum 2002)

Ideas for drugs that may be useful for the treatment and prevention of the cognitive and behavioral symptoms of Alzheimer's disease have come from a variety of sources. Clinical-pathological studies have indicated that there are a variety of brain mechanisms that may lead to or exacerbate the nerve cell dysfunction and death and loss of connections among nerve cells seen in Alzheimer's disease, including abnormal processing of proteins such as the amyloid precursor protein, beta-amyloid; oxidative damage; inflammation; and neurotrophic support of brain cells. (NIH 2002) Studies in test tubes and in animals have indicated that many of these mechanisms are potential targets for new drug discovery and development. A number of drugs targeting these mechanisms involved in Alzheimer's disease pathogenesis are currently in preclinical development or clinical testing.

Some of the drugs being investigated are new agents; others are compounds such as vitamins that are already on the market for other indications or uses, but may be effective against Alzheimer's disease. Epidemiological studies have suggested that some medications such as anti-inflammatory drugs, anti-oxidant vitamins, statins, and hormone replacement therapy may reduce the risk of developing Alzheimer's disease (NIH 2002)

One new approach to treating Alzheimer's disease is to disrupt the formation of plaques, the telltale sign of the disease. In the brains of Alzheimer's disease patients, certain proteins cleave the amyloid precursor protein (APP) into beta-amyloid fragments, which then aggregate into the characteristic plaques of the disease. Several drugs currently in development are targeted at the steps involved in this process. These include drugs that inhibit proteins that cleave the APP; a variety of agents that are proposed to inhibit the aggregation of beta-amyloid into plaques, including a plant extract from cat's claw; and immuno-therapeutic agents such as beta-amyloid vaccines. (NIH 2002)

A related strategy against Alzheimer's disease is the development of compounds proposed to be neurotrophic (i.e., facilitating the health of nerve cells) or neuroprotective against mechanisms that kill nerve cells. There are several of these types of agents in pre-clinical and clinical trials. (NIH 2002)

In addition, researchers are conducting clinical trials of drugs targeted at the behavioral symptom of agitation in people with Alzheimer's disease. Finally, substances that may protect against the development of Alzheimer's disease are in clinical trials. (NIH 2002)

Type 2 Diabetes

- Seventeen million Americans have diabetes, and over 200,000 people die each year from related complications of their disease. (CDC 2002)
- Diabetes afflicts approximately 20 percent of all Americans age 65 and older, and about one quarter of African-Americans and Hispanics over age 65.
- Clinical trials have shown that intensive control of blood glucose, blood pressure, and lipids can dramatically reduce the risk of complications.
- New approaches to diabetes management are in development that potentially will reduce the morbidity and mortality from the disease.

Percentage of Persons Age 65 & Over with Diabetes by Race/Ethnicity, 2000

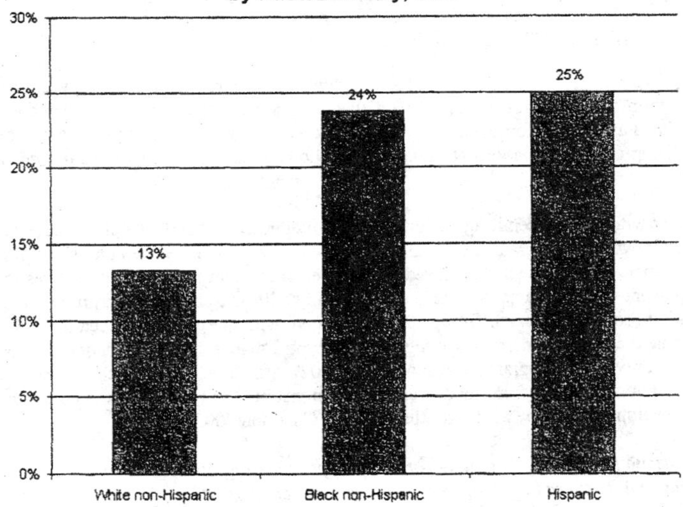

Note: Respondents were asked if they had ever been told by a doctor or other health professional that they had diabetes. Persons who said they had borderline diabetes were considered "unknown."
Source: National Health Interview Survey, 2000

Diabetes is a chronic disease of high blood glucose related to the impairment of blood glucose regulation. It can result from too little of the regulatory hormone, insulin, resistance to insulin, or both. Complications include heart disease, strokes, blindness, kidney failure, and peripheral vascular and nerve disease resulting in leg and foot amputations. Among U.S. adults, diagnosed diabetes increased 49 percent from 1990 to 2000. (CDC 2002) Diabetes disproportionately affects the elderly and certain ethnic and racial groups.

Diabetes incurs a tremendous personal, social, and financial burden. Seniors with diabetes often experience a reduced quality of life. Moreover, diabetes is an expensive disease for older Americans. In 1997, for persons aged 65 and older, total direct medical expenditures attributable to diabetes in the U.S. exceeded $32 billion. (CDC 1999) The high price of diabetes includes frequent physician and emergency room visits and admissions to hospitals and nursing homes.

Optimal treatment of diabetes can improve the quality of life and reduce health care costs. A study published in JAMA in 1998 found that treating Type 2 diabetes with a medicine to improve blood glucose (glycemic) control improved the quality of life for patients and helped keep them out of the hospital and on the job. (Testa 1998) The study also showed that patients' perceptions of their own physical and emotional health improved, while the number of bed days and hospital visits declined. Improved glycemic control can also significantly reduce the risk of developing microvascular complications (eye, kidney, and nerve disease). (CDC 2002)

Treatment and prevention for type 2 diabetes

Many patients initially control their diabetes with diet and exercise. Oral hypoglycemics are one popular form of drug treatment for type 2 diabetes. Oral hypoglycemic agents include sulfonylurea agents, metformin, and thiazolidinediones. Ultimately, most patients will require insulin. Improved formulations of insulin and methods of insulin delivery are currently in development.

Treatment with hypoglycemic agents may prevent individuals from developing diabetes. In the Diabetes Prevention Program, a clinical trial involving over 3,000 people at high risk for type 2 diabetes, diet and exercise that achieved a 5 to 7 percent weight loss reduced diabetes incidence by 58 percent in participants randomized to the study's lifestyle intervention group. (Diabetes Prevention Program Research Group 2002) Treatment with metformin reduced the risk of developing diabetes in individuals at high risk for type 2 diabetes by 31 percent over 2.8 years. (Diabetes Prevention Program Research Group 2002) Starch blockers which delay the digestion and absorption of sugars from food, were also demonstrated to cut the odds that high-risk adults would develop diabetes by 25% over three years. (Chiasson 2002)

Rosiglitazone (Avandia®) is a newer oral hypoglycemic drug approved by the FDA in 2000. This drug is not covered in Ontario, Canada or New Zealand. (Ontario Ministry of Health and Long Term Care 2001; PHARMAC 2002)

In addition to glycemic control, blood pressure control and the use of angiotensin-converting enzyme (ACE) inhibitors in people with diabetes have been demonstrated to delay the progression of kidney disease. (Golan 1999; Parving 2001; Kshirsagar 2000) Kidney failure in diabetics reduces their quality of life and often shortens their life. Treatment of diabetics with relatively inexpensive ACE inhibitors improves their quality of life and results in dramatic cost savings. (Swislocki 2001; Golan 1999)

Drugs in the pipeline for type 2 diabetes

- New drugs to target the problem of insulin resistance, which is a factor in the pathophysiology of type 2 diabetes are being investigated. (NIH, NLM 2002)

- One compound, an enzyme involved in pathways contributing to small blood vessel damage, shows promise in treating diabetic peripheral neuropathy. (United Press International 2002)

- Drugs that regulate gene expression in fat and insulin responsive tissues are also being studied. (NIH 2002)

- A compound that stimulates insulin-producing cells in the pancreas is being studied. (NIH 2002)

Type 2 diabetes generally arises from a combination of insulin resistance and inadequate production of insulin in the beta cell of the pancreas; new therapies are targeted at both of these defects. Molecular mechanisms involved in glucose toxicity underlying the development of diabetes complications have also been elucidated, yielding new targets for therapy. Moreover, scientists anticipate additional new therapeutic targets will emerge from genetic studies underway to identify genes predisposing to type 2 diabetes and to diabetes complications. (NIH 2002)

In 2002, 23 drugs were in clinical trials for the treatment and prevention of diabetes. (PhRMA 2002) Some of the agents in development are aimed at optimizing glycemic control, reducing insulin resistance, reducing obesity, and preventing the complications of diabetes. (Olefsky 2001)

Multiple pharmaceutical companies are developing new insulin sensitizing drugs for treatment or prevention of type 2 diabetes. One class of drugs acts through a nuclear receptor to regulate gene expression in fat and other insulin responsive tissues. (NIH 2002) Agents in this class have been shown to improve glucose control in type 2 diabetes, and also to delay or prevent type 2 diabetes in high-risk women with a history of gestational diabetes. Since earlier drugs in this class had significant side effects, nearly all the major pharmaceutical companies are trying to develop improved drugs that are more potent and less toxic. Several companies are investigating other mechanisms to increase insulin sensitivity (i.e. decrease insulin resistance). (NIH 2002)

Preservation or enhancement of function of the insulin producing beta cells in the pancreas is an important target for therapeutic development for diabetes. Identification of the molecular events involved in beta cell growth and development and in glucose sensing and insulin secretion by this critical cell type has important implications for therapy. (NIH 2002) Several drugs are under development based on the activity of glucagon-like peptide-1 (GLP-1) which appears to enhance growth and function of insulin producing beta cells.

Understanding of molecular mechanisms involved in glucose toxicity and development of complications of diabetes is also yielding new therapeutic strategies. For example, NIH funded research identified a key signaling molecule involved in glucose toxicity. (NIH 2002) A phase II trial of an inhibitor of this protein for treatment of diabetic peripheral neuropathy has been recently completed. Phase III trials are planned or underway using this drug to treat neuropathy (nerve damage) and it will also be studied for retinopathy, the leading cause of blindness in American adults. (NIH 2002)

Migraines

- Migraine headaches affect 28 million Americans, 75 percent of whom are women. (NIH, NINDS 2002)
- One in four households in the United States have someone affected by migraine headaches.
- Over two million seniors have migraines or severe headaches. (CDC 2002)

The most common type of vascular headache is the migraine. The cause of migraine headaches is not precisely known. It is clear that genetic factors play a role in determining who develops migraine headaches, and abnormal genes have been identified for some forms of migraine headaches. (NIH, NINDS 2002) Migraine symptoms occur in various combinations and include pain, extreme sensitivity to light and sound, nausea, and vomiting. Some individuals can predict the onset of a migraine with telltale signs that include visual disturbances, called an aura. Triggers for migraines include: lack of food or sleep, exposure to light, anxiety, stress, and hormonal irregularities.

<u>Treatment of migraine headaches</u>

There are two ways to approach the treatment of migraine headaches with drugs: prevent the attacks, or relieve symptoms after the headache occurs. Several drugs for prevention and treatment of migraines have been developed in recent years, including serotonin agonists which mimic the action of this key brain chemical. (NIH, NINDS 2002) Referred to as the triptans, these agents represent an important advance in the treatment of migraine headaches. (Goadsby 2002) Triptans selectively activate the serotonin 5-HT receptor which results in three actions: constriction of cranial blood vessels, inhibition of neurotransmitter release, and reduced transmission in nerve pain pathways. In comparison to other types of drugs for migraine headaches, triptans have distinct advantages including selective pharmacology, fewer side effects, safety and efficacy, and simple consistent pharmacokinetics. (Goadsby 2002) Triptans are not recommended for use in individuals with cardiovascular disease.

Rizatriptan benzoate (Maxalt®), a triptan, is indicated for the acute treatment of migraine headaches. *Although Maxalt® has generally been covered in private insurance plans in the U.S. for years, it is still not covered by France's state-run health-care system. (Fuhrmans 2002) Maxalt® is also not covered in New Zealand, Australia and Portugal; its use is restricted in many Canadian provinces. (see appendix)*

<u>Drugs in the pipeline for migraine headaches</u>

- Compounds that target nerves but have no vascular side effects are being tested for the treatment of migraine headaches. (Goadsby 2002)

Many of the current treatments for migraine headaches have vascular effects that produce unwanted side effects and make them contraindicated in certain subsets of patients. Since it is believed that migraine headaches primarily result from neural events that result in dilation of blood vessels, pain and further nerve stimulation, novel approaches are currently directed at nerve activation. Several neuronally active compounds are being tested. In 2001, 10 new medicines were in development for the treatment of migraine headaches. (PhRMA 2002)

CONCLUSION

Current seniors are the beneficiaries of medical innovations which have dramatically improved their quality of life in their golden years. With the recent discoveries in medical science, future breakthroughs in treating and curing chronic diseases are probable. To ensure continued progress in the fight to treat and prevent chronic disease, society must provide a nurturing environment in which research and development can flourish. Efforts to encourage medical innovations should include investing in biomedical research, protecting intellectual property rights, providing for an efficient regulatory process, and fairly compensating industry for its products.

REFERENCES

Agency for Healthcare Research and Quality (AHRQ, formerly AHCPR). Depression Guideline Panel. *Depression in primary care: volume 1. Detection and diagnosis. Clinical practice guideline, number 5.* AHCPR Publication No. 93-0550. Rockville, MD, Agency for Health Care Policy and Research, 1993.

Alzheimer's Association. Leteprinim potassium (Neotrofin®) for treating Alzheimer's. http://www.alz.org/research/clintrials/neotrofin.htm. Accessed on June 25, 2002.

Alzheimer Research Forum. Drugs in clinical trials. www.alzforum.org Accessed on July 2, 2002.

American Cancer Society. Cancer facts & figures 2002. Atlanta, GA. American Cancer Society, 2002.

American Cancer Society. Cancer vaccines show continuing improvement. May 16, 2001. http://www.cancer.org. Accessed on June 25, 2002.

American Heart Association. 2002 heart and stroke statistical update. Dallas, TX, American Heart Association. 2001.

Andersson KE, Chapple CR, Hofner K. Future drugs for the treatment of benign prostatic hyperplasia. World Journal of Urology. 19(6), 436-442, 2002.

Bellosta S, Ferri N, Bernini F, et al. Non-lipid-related effects of statins. Annals of Medicine. 32(3), 164-76, 2000.

Birkett D, Mitchell A, and McManus P. A cost-effectiveness approach to drug subsidy and pricing in Australia. Health Affairs. 20(3), 104-114, 2001.

Bombardier C, Laine L, Reicin A, et al. Comparison of upper gastrointestinal toxicity of rofecoxib and naproxen in patients with rheumatoid arthritis. VIGOR Study Group. New England Journal of Medicine. 343(21), 1520-1528, November 2000.

Boskey AL. Musculoskeletal disorders and orthopedic conditions. Journal of the American Medical Association. 285(5), 619-623, 2001.

British National Formulary (BNF). www.bnf.org. Accessed July 9, 2002.

Bumol TF, Watanabe AM. Genetic information, genomic technologies, and the future of drug discovery. Journal of the American Medical Association. 285(5), 551-555, 2001.

Burt C. National trends in the use of medications in office-based practice, 1985-1999. Health Affairs. 21(4), 206-214, July/August 2002.

Calfee, J.E. The unintended consequences of price controls. American Enterprise Institute website. www.aei.org/ra/racalfee3.htm. Accessed July 1, 2002.

Centers for Disease Control and Prevention. Healthy aging: preventing disease and improving quality of life among older Americans. www.cdc.gov/nccdphp/aag-aging.htm. Accessed on June 24, 2002.

Centers for Disease Control and Prevention. Morbidity and mortality weekly report: surveillance for asthma—United States, 1980-1999. March 29, 2002.

Centers for Disease Control and Prevention, National Center for Health Statistics. Trends in causes of death among the elderly. Aging Trends No.1. Atlanta, GA, March 2001.

Center for Disease Control and Prevention, National Center for Health Statistics. New asthma estimates: tracking prevalence, health care, and mortality. October 5, 2001. www.cdc.gov/nchs/products/pubs/pubd/hestats/asthma/asthma.htm. Accessed on July 1, 2002.

Center for Disease Control and Prevention, National Center for Health Statistics. Summary health statistics for U.S. Adults: National Health Interview Survey, 1997. CDC, Department of Health and Human Services. May 2002.

Centers for Disease Control and Prevention. Preventing heart disease and stroke: addressing the nation's leading killers. http://www.cdc.gov/nccdphp/cvdaag.htm. Accessed on June 24, 2002.

Centers for Disease Control and Prevention. Arthritis: the nation's leading cause of disability. http://www.cdc.gov/nccdphp/arthritis. Accessed on June 24, 2002.

Centers for Disease Control and Prevention. Diabetes: disabling, deadly, and on the rise. http://www.cdc.gov/diabetes/pubs/glance.htm. Accessed on June 24, 2002.

Centers for Disease Control and Prevention. National Center for Chronic Disease Prevention and Health Promotion. Preventing the diseases of aging. Chronic Disease Notes & Reports. 12(3),1999.

Chiasson J-L, Josse RG, Gomis R, et al. Acarbose for prevention of type 2 diabetes mellitus: the STOP-NIDDM randomized trial. Lancet. 359, 2072-2077, 2002.

Crystal RG. Research opportunities and advances in lung disease. Journal of the American Medical Association. 285(5), 612-618, 2001.

Cutler DM, McClellan M. Is technological change in medicine worth it? The Value of Rx Innovation: A Primer. Health Affairs. Pages 1-19, 2001.

Davidson, S. Quicker drug approvals on the way for Europe. Nature Biotechnology. Nature Publishing Group. 10, 798-799, September 2001.

de Grooth GJ, Kuivenhoven JA, Stalenhoef AF, et al. Efficacy and safety of a novel cholesteryl ester transfer protein inhibitor, JTT-705, in humans: a randomized phase II dose-response study. Circulation. 105(18), 2159-65, 2002.

Diabetes Prevention Program Research Group. Reduction in the incidence of type 2 diabetes with lifestyle intervention or metformin. New England Journal of Medicine. 346(6), 393-403, 2002.

Dykes, L. Why price controls are the wrong prescription. Pacific Research Institute. June 13, 2001. www.pacificresearch.org/pub/act/2001/act_01-06-13a.html. Accessed July 1, 2002.

Ettinger B, Black DM, Mitlak BH, et al. Reduction of vertebral fracture risk in postmenopausal women with osteoporosis treated with raloxifene: results from a 3-year randomized clinical trial. Multiple Outcomes of Raloxifene Evaluation (MORE) Investigators. Journal of the American Medical Association. 282(22), 2124, 1999.

Europe Economics. Access to important new medicines: where and why do patients wait? Europe Economics. London, UK. 2000.

European Commission. High level group on innovation and provision of medicines: recommendations for action. European Communities. Brussels, Belgium. May 7, 2002.

Evenson B. Health Canada finally approves lymphoma drug: Rituxan an effective anti-cancer agent with few side-effects. National Post. April 5, 2000.

Fagan SC, Morgenstern LB, Petitta A, et al. Cost-effectiveness of tissue plasminogen activator for acute ischemic stroke. Neurology. 50(4), 883, 1998.

Federal Interagency Forum on Aging-Related Statistics. Older Americans 2000: key indicators of well-being. Federal Interagency Forum on Aging-Related Statistics. Washington, DC, US Government Printing Office, 2000.

Freedman VA, Aykan H, Martin, LG. Another look at aggregate changes in severe cognitive impairment. Journal of Gerontology. Series B, Psychological Sciences and Social Sciences. 56(2), S100-11, 2002.

Freedman VA, Martin, LG. Contribution of chronic conditions to aggregate changes in old-age functioning. American Journal of Public Health. 90(11), 1755-60, 2000.

Freedman VA, Martin, LG. Understanding trends in functional limitations among older Americans. American Journal of Public Health. 88(10), 1457-62, 1998.

Fuhrmans V, Naik G. In Europe, drug makers fight against mandatory price cuts. The Wall Street Journal. June 7, 2002.

Gambardella A, Orsenigo L, Pammolli F. Global competativeness in pharmaceuticals, a European perspective. Report prepared for Enterprise Directorate-General of the European Commission. European Communities. 2001.

Gawchik SM, Saccar CL. Role of antileukotriene agents in asthma therapy. Journal of the American Osteopathic Association. 100(1), 32, 37-43, January 2000.

Goadsby PJ, Lipton RB, Ferrari MD. Migraine—current understanding and treatment. New England Journal of Medicine. 346(4), 257-268, 2002.

Golan L, Birkmeyer JD, Welch HG. The cost-effectiveness of treating all patients with type 2 diabetes with Angiotensin-converting enzyme inhibitors. Annals of Internal Medicine. 131(9), 660-667, 1999.

Hansel TT, Barnes PJ. Novel drugs for treating asthma. Current Allergy and Asthma Reports. 1(2), 164-173, 2001.

Hawkes N. Patients are denied life-saving cancer drug. London Times. May 28, 2002.

Health Canada Online. Drug product database. www.hc-sc.gc.ca/hpb-dgps/therapeut/htmleng/dpd.html. Accessed on July 9, 2002.

Hoyert DL, Kochanek KD, Murphy SL. Deaths: final data for 1997. National Vital Statistics Report, 47(19). DHHS Publication No. 99-1120. Hyattsville, MD: National Center for Health Statistics, 1999.

Koopman WJ. Prospects for autoimmune disease: research advances in rheumatoid arthritis. Journal of the American Medical Association . 285(5), 648-650, 2001.

Kremer, M. Creating markets for new vaccines part II: design issues. NBER working paper 7717. National Bureau of Economic Research. Cambridge, MA. May 2000.

Kshirsagar AV, Joy MS, Hogan SL, et al. Effect of ACE inhibitors in diabetic and nondiabetic chronic renal disease: a systematic overview of randomized placebo-controlled trials. American Journal of Kidney Disease. 35(4), 297-307, 2000.

Lawrence, F. The battle over immunization. The Guardian. London, U.K. http://www.guardian.co.uk/medicalscience/story/0,1129,541949,00.html. Accessed July 2, 2002.

Lefkowitz RJ, Willerson JT. Prospects for cardiovascular research. Journal of the American Medical Association. 285(5), 581-587, 2001.

Leitersdorf E. Selective cholesterol absorption inhibition: a novel strategy in lipid-lowering management. International Journal of Clinical Practice. 56(2), 116-119, March 2002.

Lewin Group. The impact of the Canadian system on access to new medical technology including prescription drugs. The Lewin Group. March 7, 2000.

Lichtenberg FR, Are the benefits of newer drugs worth their costs? Evidence from the 1996 MEPS. The Value of Rx Innovation: A Primer. Health Affairs, pages 21-31. 2001.

Lipworth BJ. Leukotriene-receptor antagonists. Lancet. 353(9146), 57-62, 1999.

Livingston DM, Shivdasani R. Toward mechanism-based cancer care. Journal of the American Medical Association . 285(5), 588-593, 2001.

Margolin K. Inhibition of vascular endothelial growth factor in the treatment of solid tumors. Current Oncology Reports. 4(1), 20-8, 2001.

McClung MR, Geusens P, Miller PD, et al. Effect of risedronate on the risk of hip fracture in elderly women. New England Journal of Medicine. 344(5), 333-340, 2001.

Merck & Co. E-mail communication to the Office of the Assistant Secretary for Planning and Evaluation, Department of Health and Human Services. June 28, 2002.

Mulrow CD, Williams JW Jr., Trivedi M, et al. Evidence report on treatment of depression-newer pharmacotherapies. Psychopharmacology Bulletin. 34(4), 409-795, 1998.

Murray CJL, Lopez AD, eds. Summary: the global burden of disease: a comprehensive assessment of mortality and disability from diseases, injuries, and risk factors in 1990 and projected to 2020. Cambridge, MA; published by the Harvard School of Public Health on behalf of the World Health Organization and the World Bank, Harvard University Press, 1996.

Narrow WE. One-year prevalence of depressive disorders among adults 18 and over in the U.S.: NIMH ECA prospective data. Population estimates based on U.S. Census estimated residential population age 18 and over on July 1, 1998. Unpublished. Accessed on June 24, 2002. http://www.nimh.nih.gov/pubicat/elderydepsuicide.cfm.

National Institute for Clinical Excellence. (NICE) Press releases. www.nice.org.uk. Accessed on July 9, 2002.

National Institutes of Health. Medications under development for the treatment of seniors. E-mail communication. June 27, 2002.

National Institutes of Health. New agents in development. E-mail communication. July 2, 2002.

National Institutes of Health, National Library of Medicine. Cholesterol. Medline Plus Health Information Database. www.nih.nlm/medlineplus/ Accessed on June 24, 2002.

National Institutes of Health, National Heart, Lung and Blood Institute. Cholesterol Lowering Medicines. http://rover.nhlbi.nih.gov/chd/meds.htm Accessed on June 24, 2002.

National Institutes of Health, National Cancer Institute. Annual report shows overall decline in U.S. cancer death rates; cancer burden is expected to rise with an aging population. May 14, 2002. http://newscenter.cancer.gov/pressreleases/2002reportnation.html. Accessed June 24, 2002.

National Institutes of Health, NIDDK. Prostatic enlargement: benign prostatic hyperplasia. www.niddk.nih.gov/health/urolog/pubs/prostate/index.htm. Accessed on July 1, 2002.

National Institutes of Health, National Institute of Neurological Disorders and Stroke. Headache—hope through research. www.ninds.nih.gov/health_and_medical/pubs/headache_htr.htm?format=printable. Accessed July 1, 2002.

National Institutes of Health, National Institute of Neurological Disorders and Stroke. Migraine update. www.ninds.nih.gov/health_and_medical/pubs/migraineupdate.htm?format=printable. Accessed July 1, 2002.

National Institutes of Health, National Institute of Neurological Disorders and Stroke t-PA Stroke Study Group. Tissue plasminogen activator for acute ischemic stroke. New England Journal of Medicine. 333(24), 1581-1587, 1995.

National Institutes of Health, National Library of Medicine. Diabetes mellitus, non-insulin-dependent. http://www.clinicaltrials.gov. Accessed on June 25, 2002.

National Institutes of Health. Osteoporosis and Related Bone Diseases, National Resource Center. Osteoporosis overview. http://www.osteo.org/osteo.html. Accessed on June 24, 2002.

National Institutes of Health, National Library of Medicine, National Institute of Diabetes and Digestive and Kidney Disease. Clinical alert: diet and exercise dramatically delay type 2 diabetes; diabetes medication metformin also effective. August 8, 2001. http://www.nlm.nih.gov/databases/alerts/diabetes01.html. Accessed on June 24, 2002.

National Osteoporosis Foundation. Patient Info: medications and osteoporosis. http://www.nof.org/patientinfo/medications.htm. Accessed on June 24, 2002.

Neumann PJ, Sandberg EI, Bell CM, et al. Are pharmaceuticals cost effective? A review of the evidence. Health Affairs. 19(2),92-109, 2001.

New Zealand Guidelines Group. Guidelines for the support and management of people with dementia: cognition of enhancing drug treatments in dementia. Enigma Publishing Limited. 2002. http://www.nzgg.org.nz/library/gl_complete/dementia/treatment.cfm. Accessed July 9, 2002.

Olefsky JM. Prospects for research in diabetes mellitus. Journal of the American Medical Association. 285(5), 628-632, 2001.

Ontario Ministry of Health and Long Term Care. Ontario drug benefit formulary, number 37. March 7, 2001. www.gov.on.ca/health/english/program/drugs/obdf_mn.html. Accessed on July 9, 2002.

Pacher P, Kohogyi E, Kecskemeti V, et al. Current trends in the development of new antidepressants. Current Medicinal Chemistry. 8,89-100, 2001.

Paget SA. Efficacy of anakinra in bone: comparison to other biologics. Advances in Therapy. 19(1), 27-39, 2002.

Parving HH, Hovind P, Rossing K, et al. Evolving strategies for renoprotection: diabetic nephropathy. Current Opinion Nephrology and Hypertension. 10(4), 515-522, 2001.

Pharmaceutical Management Agency (PHARMAC). New Zealand pharmaceutical schedule. www.pharmac.govt.nz. Accessed on July 9, 2002.

Pharmaceutical Research and Manufacturers of America (PhRMA). 2002 Survey: new medicines in development for older Americans. www.phrma.org. Accessed July 9, 2002.

Pharmaceutical Research and Manufacturers of America (PhRMA). Online clinical trials database, respiratory disorders, asthma. www.phrma.org. Accessed July 2, 2002.

Pharmaceutical Research and Manufacturers of America (PhRMA). New medicines in development for neurologic disorders. www.phrma.org. Accessed July 2, 2002.

Pharmaceutical Research and Manufacturers of America (PhRMA). Selected medicines in development for heart disease and stroke. January 2002. www.phrma.org. Accessed June 24, 2002.

Pharmaceutical Research and Manufacturers of America (PhRMA). Selected drugs in development for cancer. January 2002. www.phrma.org. Accessed June 24, 2002.

Quebec Prescription Drug Insurance Plan. List of medications. www.ramq.gouv.qc.ca/crc/eng/cit/assmed/cond.shtml. Accessed on July 9, 2002.

Sabatine MS, Jang I-K. The use of glycoprotein IIb/IIIa inhibitors in patients with coronary artery disease. American Journal of Medicine. 109, 224-237, 2000.

Sherman DG, Atkinson RP, Chippendale T, et al. Intravenous ancrod for treatment of acute ischemic stroke: the STAT study: a randomized controlled trial. Stroke Treatment with Ancrod Trial. Journal of the American Medical Association. 283(18), 2395-403, 2000.

Sliverstein FE, Faich G, Goldstein JL, et al. Gastrointestinal toxicity with celecoxib vs nonsteroidal anti-inflammatory drugs for osteoarthritis and rheumatoid arthritis: the CLASS study: A randomized controlled trial. Celecoxib Long-term Arthritis Safety Study. Journal of the American Medical Association. 284(10), 1247-55, September 2000.

Slamon DJ, Leyland-Jones B, Shak S, et al. Use of chemotherapy plus a monoclonal antibody against HER2 for metastatic breast cancer that overexpresses HER2. New England Journal of Medicine. 344(11), 783-792, 2001.

Swislocki AL, Siegel D. Renal effects of Angiotensin-converting enzyme inhibitors that result in cost savings and improved patient outcomes. American Journal Managed Care. 7(3), 283-295, 2001.

Szelenyi I. Asthma therapy in the new millennium. Inflammation Research. 51(6),273-282, 2002.

Tajima O. Mental health care in Japan: recognition and treatment of depression and anxiety disorders. Journal of Clinical Psychiatry. 62(suppl 13), 39-44, 2001.

Testa MA, Simonson DC. Health economic benefits and quality of life during improved glycemic control in patients with type 2 diabetes mellitus. Journal of the American Medical Association. 280(17), 1490-1496, 1998.

Tobias JH, Flanagan AM, Scutt AM, Novel therapeutic targets in osteoporosis. Expert Opinion on Therapeutic Targets. 6(1),41-56, 2002.

Tufts Center for the Study of Drug Development. How new drugs move through the development and approval process. 2001. http://www.csdd.tufts.edu/NewsEvents/RecentNews.asp?newsid=4. Accessed June 28, 2002.

United Nations. World population aging: 1950-2050. United Nations. New York, NY. 2002.

United Press International. 'Breakthrough' diabetes drug tested. June 18, 2002. http://www.nlm.nih.gov/medlineplus/news/fullstory_8144.html. Accessed on June 24, 2002.

United States International Trade Commission. Pricing of Prescription Drugs. United States International Trade Commission. Publication 3333. December 2000.

University of Washington School of Medicine. OsteoEd website http://osteoed.org/cases/overview.html. Accessed on June 27, 2002.

Walker, M. Wilson, G. Waiting your turn: hospital waiting lists in Canada. Fraser Institute. Eleventh edition. September 2001.

Wall Street Journal. Cancer-gene drugs flourish, yielding hope, but no quick fix. May 16, 2002.

Weinstein JN. Pharmacogenomics - teaching old drugs new tricks. New England Journal of Medicine. 343(19), 1408-1409, 2000.

World Intellectual Property Organization (WIPO). Discussion paper. Policy Advisory Task Force Meeting. Beijing, China. May 22, 2002.

Appendix
Selected FDA Approved Drugs and Biologics with Restricted Access in Other Countries

There are several drugs currently in clinical trials for treatment of BPH. (PhRMA 2002) New approaches for the treatment of BPH and resulting urinary tract symptoms are being investigated. (Andersson 2002) These new approaches target sites both within and exterior to the prostate gland. By their effect on the smooth muscle in the bladder wall, muscarinic receptor antagonists may reduce the urinary urgency and frequency associated with BPH. Endothelin receptor antagonists may prevent cell proliferation in both the prostate gland and the bladder. Moreover, these agents may also affect muscle contraction in the bladder wall, decreasing some of the symptoms of BPH. In addition, drugs directed at specific subtypes of alpha-1 adrenoceptors may prove more effective and tolerable than nonselective compounds.

Depression

- An estimated six percent of Americans ages 65 and older in a given year (approximately 2 million of the 34 million adults in this age group in 1998), have a diagnosable depressive illness (major depressive disorder, bipolar disorder, or dysthymic disorder). (Narrow 1998)

- As a result of depression, older Americans are disproportionately likely to commit suicide. Although they comprise only 13 percent of the U.S. population, individuals ages 65 and older accounted for 19 percent of all suicide deaths in 1997. (Hoyert, 1999)

- New effective treatments, with fewer undesirable side-effects, are available for depression.

Major depression is a leading cause of disability in the United States and worldwide. (Murray 1996) In contrast to the normal emotional experiences of sadness, grief, loss, or passing mood states, depressive disorders can be extreme and persistent and can significantly interfere with an individual's ability to function, robbing one of the joy of living. Depression often co-occurs with other illnesses such as cardiovascular disease, stroke, diabetes, and cancer, which have a significant incidence in seniors. (AHRQ, formerly AHCPR 1993) When depression co-occurs with medical conditions, it can interfere with the patient's ability to follow the necessary treatment regimen or to participate in a rehabilitation program. It may also increase impairment from the medical disorder and impede its improvement.

Treatment of depression

Antidepressant medications are widely used effective treatments for depression. (Mulrow 1998) Existing antidepressant drugs are known to influence the functioning of certain neurotransmitters in the brain, primarily serotonin and norepinephrine. Older medications—tricyclic antidepressants and monoamine oxidase inhibitors—affect the activity of both of these neurotransmitters simultaneously. The disadvantage of these older medications is that they can be difficult to tolerate due to side effects or dietary and/or medication restrictions. Newer medications, such as the selective serotonin reuptake inhibitors (SSRIs), have significantly fewer side effects than older drugs, making it easier for patients, including older adults, to adhere to treatment. The anti-depressant effect of SSRIs is presumed to be linked to their inhibition of

Appendix
Selected FDA Approved Drugs and Biologics with Restricted Access in Other Countries

Indication	Product	Market*	Nature of Government Plan Restriction**	Comment
Acne	Azelaic acid (Azelex)	Canada	Not Approved	Not approved for use by Health Canada. (FDA approved 9/13/95)
Alzheimer's	Donepezil (Aricept)	Ontario, Canada	Restricted Coverage	Coverage is restricted to patients who have mild to moderate Alzheimer's and have demonstrated benefit after 3 months of treatment.
		Quebec, Canada	Not Covered	Not listed on Quebec's prescription drug formulary.
		New Zealand	Not Covered	Not approved for coverage by PHARMAC of New Zealand.
Allergies	Azelastine (Astelin)	Canada	Not Approved	Not approved for use by Health Canada. (FDA approved 11/1/96)
	Pemirolast (Alamast)	Canada	Not Approved	Not approved for use by Health Canada. (FDA approved 9/24/99)
Amyotrophic Lateral Sclerosis	Riluzole (Rilutek)	Canada	Not Covered	Riluzole has not been approved for use in Canada.[1]
Arthritis/Pain	Celecoxib (Celebrex)	Ontario, Canada	Restricted Coverage	Coverage is restricted to patients with arthritis who have failed an adequate trial of other pain medications and have a history of ulcer or gastro-intestinal bleeding.
		New Zealand	Not Covered	Not covered for use by PHARMAC of New Zealand.
	Etanercept (Enbrel)	Britain	Restricted Coverage	Britain's National Health Service (NHS) covers etanercept only as a second line therapy for children aged 4-17 with non-responsive arthritis in at least 5 joints and in adults with active rheumatoid arthritis who are nonresponsive to other medications.
		Japan	Not Approved	Not approved for use in Japan.
		Ontario, Canada	Not Covered	Not listed on Ontario's prescription drug formulary.
		New Zealand	Not Covered	Not covered for use by PHARMAC of New Zealand.
	Infliximab (Remicade)	Britain	Restricted Coverage	Britain's NHS covers infliximab only as a second line therapy in combination with methotrexate for adults with active rheumatoid arthritis who are not responsive to other medications.
		Ontario, Canada	Not Covered	Not listed on Ontario's prescription drug formulary.
		New Zealand	Not Covered	Not covered for use by PHARMAC of New Zealand.

[1] ALS Society of Canada. Drug Trials. www.als.ca/manual-whatisals-drugtrials.shtml Accessed on July 8, 2002.

* This table is not intended to be a comprehensive list of markets where access to selected medications is limited. There may be additional countries/markets that restrict access to the medications listed.

** Sources include government websites, reports in news media, communications with pharmaceutical manufacturers, peer-reviewed literature and other sources. See the final page of the appendix for a list of government websites used as source material. Not all examples have been independently verified for all countries listed.

Indication	Product	Market	Nature of Government Plan Restriction	Comment
	Rofecoxib (Vioxx)	New Zealand	Not Covered	Available since March 2000, but not approved for coverage by PHARMAC.
		Australia	Restricted Coverage	Coverage is restricted to symptomatic treatment of patients with osteoarthritis
		British Columbia, Canada	Restricted Coverage	Coverage is restricted to patients who have failed to benefit from acetaminophen and at least three other funded non-steroidal anti-inflammatory drugs (NSAIDs).
		New Brunswick and Saskatchewan, Canada	Restricted Coverage	Coverage is restricted to patients who meet one of the following criteria: age 65+, past history of ulcers, concurrent warfarin therapy, concurrent prednisone therapy, or failure or intolerance to at least two other NSAIDs.
		Ontario, Canada	Restricted Coverage	Coverage is restricted to a maximum daily dose of 25 mg for the treatment of osteoarthritis. Prior therapy with acetaminophen for several weeks must have failed, and the patient must have a history of documented clinically significant ulcer or GI bleed, or failure or intolerance to at least three NSAIDs.
	Tramadol (Ultram)	Canada	Not Approved	Not approved for use by Health Canada. (FDA approved 3/3/95)
Asthma	Montelukast (Singulair)	New Zealand	Not Covered	Available since 1998, but not covered.
		Australia	Not Covered	Currently not covered, but negotiations for listing are on-going.
		Belgium	Not Covered	Available, but not covered.
		Finland	Not Covered	Pediatric strengths are available, but not covered.
		British Columbia, Canada	Not Covered	Coverage was restricted in 1999 and discontinued in 2001
		Newfoundland, Canada	Restricted Coverage	Coverage is restricted to patients uncontrolled on therapeutic doses of inhaled corticosteroids who have failed to respond to or have a contraindication to zafirlukast.
		Nova Scotia, Canada	Restricted Coverage	Coverage is restricted to 4 and 5 mg chewable format for patients younger than 12.
		Ontario and New Brunswick, Canada	Not Covered	Available, but not covered. Not listed on formulary.
		Prince Edward Island, Canada	Restricted Coverage	Coverage is restricted to patients on concurrent steroid therapy or patients not well controlled with inhaled corticosteroids.
		Saskatchewan, Canada	Restricted Coverage	Coverage is restricted to patients with Special Authorization for adjunctive treatment of asthma who are not well controlled with inhaled corticosteroids.
	Zileuton (Zyflo)	Canada	Not Approved	Not approved for use by Health Canada. (FDA approved 12/9/96)

Indication	Product	Market	Nature of Government Plan Restriction	Comment
Benign Prostatic Hyperplasia	Finasteride (Proscar)	New Zealand	Not Covered	Available, but not listed on formulary. (FDA approved 3/20/98)
		Ontario, Canada	Not Covered	Not listed on Ontario's prescription drug formulary.
Cancer	Bexarotene (Targretin)	Canada	Not Approved	Not approved for use by Health Canada. (FDA approved 12/29/99)
		Japan	Not Approved	Not approved for use in Japan.
		New Zealand	Not Approved	Not approved for use by Medsafe of New Zealand. (FDA approved 12/29/99)
	Imatinib (Gleevec or Glivec)	Britain	Restricted Coverage	In a preliminary assessment of imatinib prepared for Britain's National Institute for Clinical Excellence (NICE), it is recommended that imatinib only be used for treatment of accelerated phase of chronic myeloid leukemia and not for the routine treatment of the chronic or blast crisis stages. This is a preliminary recommendation that has not yet been finalized.
		New Zealand	Not Covered	Not covered for use by PHARMAC of New Zealand.
	Interlukin-2	Canada	Restricted Coverage	Interlukin-2 is generally not covered in Canada for treatment of metastatic kidney cancer.[2]
	Irinotecan (Camptosar)	Britain	Restricted Coverage	Britain's NHS restricts irinotecan coverage, either alone or in combination, as a first-line treatment for colorectal cancer. Reimbursement for this drug is permitted if other treatments fail.
		New Zealand	Not Covered	Available, but not covered.[3]
	Oxaliplatin (Eloxatin)	Britain	Restricted Coverage	Britain's NHS restricts coverage for oxaliplatin as a first-line treatment for colorectal cancer, except in patients whose cancer has spread to the liver and may become operable with treatment. Reimbursement for this drug is permitted if other treatments fail.
	Rituximab (Rituxan)	Britain	Restricted Coverage	Britain's NHS restricts coverage of rituximab to last-line treatment for stage 3 or 4 non-Hodgkin's lymphoma. Reimbursement for rituximab is permitted only after conventional chemotherapy agents have failed.
		Ontario, Canada	Not Covered	Not listed on Ontario's drug formulary.
		New Zealand	Not Covered	Not covered for use by PHARMAC of New Zealand.
	Tratuzumab (Herceptin)	Britain	Restricted Coverage	Britain's NHS restricts coverage of tratuzumab to women with advanced HER2 positive breast cancer who meet specific clinical criteria.
	Raltitrexed (Tomudex)	Britain	Not Covered	Britain's NHS restricts does not cover raltitrexed for use outside of appropriately designed clinical studies.

[2] Cancer Guide. Steve Dunn's Kidney Cancer Page. www.cancerguide.org/kidney.html Accessed on July 8, 2002.
[3] The Daily News (New Plymouth). Society outraged at cancer drug funding. May 19, 2001.

Indication	Product	Market	Nature of Government Plan Restriction	Comment
Cancer Continued...	Other new cancer drugs	Austrailia	Delays in Approval	In Austrailia, cancer treatment drugs take 3.5 times as long to approve as anti-HIV therapies. The Therapeutic Goods Administration (TGA) is markedly slower than the U.S. FDA in getting both groups of medications on the market.[4]
		New Zealand	Not Covered	In four of New Zealand's six regional cancer centers, patients have been denied access to new cancer treatments due to lack of funding in the regional health care system.[5]
Crohn's Disease	Infliximab (Remicade)	Japan	Unavailable	
Cushing's Syndrome	Corticorelin (Acthrel)	Canada	Not Approved	Not approved for use by Health Canada. (FDA approved 5/23/96)
Depression	Bupropion (Wellbutrin)	Canada	Restricted Coverage	Covered as a limited use benefit only in patients who are unresponsive to other antidepressants under Health Canada's Non-Insured Health Benefits Program.
	Fluvoxamine (Luvox)	New Zealand	Not Covered	Not approved for coverage by PHARMAC of New Zealand.
	All SSRI's	Japan	Delays in Approval	The first SSRI marketed in Japan, fluvoxamine, was launched in 1999.[6] SSRI's were first approved for sale by the FDA in 1987.
Diabetes	Rosiglitazone (Avandia)	Ontario, Canada	Not Covered	Not listed on Ontario's prescription drug formulary.
		New Zealand	Not Covered	Not approved for coverage by PHARMAC of New Zealand.
End Stage Renal Disease (ESRD)	Selvamer (Renagel)	Japan	Not Approved	Not approved for use in Japan
		New Zealand	Not Approved	Not approved for use by Medsafe of New Zealand. (FDA approved 11/2/98)
Fetal Respiratory Distress	Poractant Alpha (Curosurf)	Canada	Not Approved	Not approved for use by Health Canada. (FDA approved 11/18/99)
GI and Ulcer	Amlexanax (Aphthasol)	Canada	Not Approved	Not approved for use by Health Canada. (FDA approved 12/17/96)
	Omeprazole (Prilosec)	Canada	Restricted Coverage	Implementation of resource based pricing caused physicians to replace omeprazole with cimetidine, which is less effective in preventing gastric bleeding

[4] The Mercury Hobart. Alarm at cancer drug lag. December 2, 2000.
[5] The Dominion (Wellington). Cancer patients miss out on new drugs. May 12, 2001.
[6] Tajima O. Mental health care in Japan: recognition and treatment of depression and anxiety disorders. Journal of Clinical Psychiatry. 62(suppl 13), 39-44, 2001.

Indication	Product	Market	Nature of Government Plan Restriction	Comment
GI and Ulcer Continued...	Rabeprazole (Aciphex)	Canada	Not Approved	Not approved for use by Health Canada. (FDA approved 8/19/99)
High Cholesterol	Simvastatin (Zocor)	New Zealand	Restricted Coverage prior to Feb. 2001	Until the expiration of simvastatin's patent, coverage for simvastatin was restricted to patients with a >20%, 5-year risk of cardiovascular disease who met minimum cholesterol thresholds.
		Australia	Restricted Coverage	Coverage restrictions are complex, including the failure of 6 weeks prior dietary therapy.
	Atorvastatin (Lipitor)	New Zealand	Restricted Coverage	As of July 1, 2002, coverage of lipitor is restricted to patients who receive special authority approval from the government. Patients who have not approved special authority must switch to an alternate statin.
	Lovastatin (Mevacor)	New Zealand	Not Covered	Not covered for use by PHARMAC of New Zealand.
	Pravastatin (Pravachol)	New Zealand	Not Covered	Not covered for use by PHARMAC of New Zealand.
Hyperpara-thyroidism	Paricalcitol (Zemplar)	Canada	Not Approved	Not approved for use by Health Canada. (FDA approved 4/17/98)
Hypertension	Fenoldopam (Corlopam)	Canada	Not Approved	Not approved for use by Health Canada. (FDA approved 9/23/97)
	Losartan Potassium (Cozaar)	New Zealand	Restricted Coverage	Only specialists (cardiologists) can initiate therapy, and then only if the patient suffers from congestive heart failure and treatment attempts with at least two types of ACE inhibitors have not been tolerated.
		Australia	Not Covered	The product was covered approximately 6 years ago, but the government instituted a reference price/reimbursement limit that was commercially unacceptable. It is no longer offered on the market.
		Canada (British Columbia, Ontario, New Brunswick, Newfoundland)	Restricted Coverage	Generally restricted to patients who cannot tolerate ACE inhibitors.
	Losartan Potassium/ hydrochloro-thiazide (Hyzaar)	British Columbia, Canada	Restricted Coverage	Coverage is restricted to patients who have experienced a cough with ACE inhibitors and also require a diuretic.
		New Brunswick, and Newfoundland, Canada	Restricted Coverage	A "special authorization" may be considered if the doctor justifies the need. There are no published criteria.

Indication	Product	Market	Nature of Government Plan Restriction	Comment
Hypertension Continued...	Losartan Potassium/ hydrochloro-thiazide (Hyzaar) Continued...	Ontario, Canada	Restricted Coverage	Coverage is restricted to patients who cannot tolerate beta-blockers or in whom beta-blockers and diuretics alone are not effective; and who have experienced adverse effects with ACE inhibitors, and who require the addition of a diuretic to achieve adequate hypertension control.
	Moexipril (Univasc)	Canada	Not Approved	Not approved for use by Health Canada. (FDA approved 4/19/95)
	Nisoldipine (Sular)	Canada	Not Approved	Not approved for use by Health Canada. (FDA approved 2/2/95)
	Valsartan (Diovan)	Ontario, Canada	Restricted Coverage	Restricted to patients who cannot tolerate diuretics, beta-blockers, and ACE inhibitors.
		New Zealand	Not Covered	Not approved for coverage by PHARMAC of New Zealand.
	Enalapril mal-eate/HCTZ (Vaseretic)	British Columbia, Canada	Restricted Coverage	Coverage is listed as a "partial benefit" under Pharmacare's Reference Drug Pricing (RDP) program.
Infectious Disease	Albendazole (Albenza)	Canada	Not Approved	Not approved for use by Health Canada. (FDA approved 6/11/96)
	Ivermectin (Stromectol)	Canada	Not Approved	Not approved for use by Health Canada. (FDA approved 11/22/96)
	Rifapentine (Priftin)	Canada	Not Approved	Not approved for use by Health Canada. (FDA approved 6/22/98)
Insomnia	Zaleplon (Sonata)	Canada	Not Approved	Not approved for use by Health Canada. (FDA approved 8/13/99)
Eye Disorders	Dorzolamide (Trusopt)	New Zealand	Restricted Coverage	Specialist required to initiate therapy, and restricted only to patients with primary open-angle glaucoma with very high intra-ocular pressure that cannot be controlled using other therapies.
	Loteprednol (Lotemax)	Canada	Not Approved	Not approved for use by Health Canada. (FDA approved 3/9/98)
Migraine Headache	Rizatriptan (Maxalt)	New Zealand	Not Covered	Available since 1999, but not approved for use by PHARMAC.
		Australia	Not Covered	Not available.
		Belgium	Not Covered	Available, but not covered.
		France	Not Covered	Not available.
		Portugal	Not Covered	Available, but without reimbursement.
		Alberta, Canada	Restricted Coverage	Coverage is restricted to patients 18-24 years of age for treatment of acute migraine attacks where standard therapy has failed. Special authorization is required for treatment of acute migraine attacks in patients 65+ where standard therapy has failed and for those who were using Maxalt prior to turning 65.

Indication	Product	Market	Nature of Government Plan Restriction	Comment
Migraine Headache Continued...	Rizatriptan (Maxalt) Continued...	Nova Scotia, Canada	Restricted Coverage	Coverage is restricted to patients experiencing moderate migraines (if other therapies have not been effective) or severe migraines.
		Ontario, Canada	Not Covered	Not listed on Ontario's prescription drug formulary.
		Saskatchewan, Canada	Restricted Coverage	Coverage is restricted to patients when other standard therapies, such as analgesics and/or ergotamine, have failed. Eligibility is restricted to beneficiaries 18-65 years of age.
Multiple Sclerosis (MS)	• -Interferon (Avonex, Betaseron) Glatiramer acetate (Copaxone)	Britain	Not Covered	Britain's NHS does not cover • -Interferon and glatiramer acetate for the treatment of MS.
Osteoporosis	Alendronate (Fosamax)	New Zealand	Restricted Coverage	Only specialists can initiate this therapy, and then only if the patient has suffered one previous, significant osteoporotic vertebral or hip fracture (radiologically demonstrated).
		Australia	Restricted Coverage	Coverage is restricted to patients who have sustained a fracture due to minimal trauma and established the existence of osteoporosis.
		Belgium	Restricted Coverage	Coverage is restricted to patients with fracture or low bone density.
		France	Restricted Coverage	Coverage is restricted to patients with fracture.
		Italy	Restricted Coverage	Coverage is restricted to patients with vertebral or hip fracture.
		Alberta, Canada	Restricted Coverage	Coverage is restricted to patients with vertebral of other fractures. Special authorization is granted for 24 months.
		British Columbia, Canada	Restricted Coverage	Coverage is restricted to patients who have fractures due to osteoporosis, and an adequate trial of etidronate (at least one year) that has failed to prevent fractures.
		Newfoundland, Canada	Restricted Coverage	Coverage is restricted to patients with low bone mass or fractures, or women who have failed or are intolerant to hormone replacement therapy (HRT).
		Nova Scotia, Canada	Restricted Coverage	Coverage is restricted to patients who have a fracture, and have failed HRT. Other restrictions also apply.
		Ontario, Canada	Restricted Coverage	Coverage is restricted to postmenopausal women who have failed to respond to etidronate or experienced fracture during etidronate therapy
		Saskatchewan, Canada	Restricted Coverage	Coverage is restricted to patients who have not responded to etidtronate or didrocal and have new fractures or Paget's disease.
	Raloxifene (Evistia)	Ontario, Canada	Restricted Coverage	Coverage is restricted to patients who have failed to respond to etidronate or experienced a new fracture
		Quebec, Canada	Not Covered	Not listed on Quebec's prescription drug formulary
		New Zealand	Not Covered	Not covered for use by PHARMAC of New Zealand

Indication	Product	Market	Nature of Government Plan Restriction	Comment
Reproductive Health	Ganirelix Acetate (Antagon)	Canada	Not Approved	Not approved for use by Health Canada. (FDA approved 7/29/99)
Seizures	Levetirace-tam (Keppra)	Canada	Not Approved	Not approved for use by Health Canada. (FDA approved 11/30/99)
	Tiagabine (Gabitril)	Canada	Not Approved	Not approved for use by Health Canada. (FDA approved 9/30/97)
Vascular Disease	Cilostazol (Pletal)	Canada	Not Approved	Not approved for use by Health Canada. (FDA approved 1/15/99)

Sources:

Canada

Health Canada. Non-insured Health Benefits Drug Benefit List. www.hc-sc.gc.ca/fnihb/nihb/index.htm Accessed on July 9, 2002.

Health Canada Online. Drug Product Database. www.hc-sc.gc.ca/hpb-dgps/therapeut/htmleng/dpd.html Accessed on July 9, 2002.

Ontario Ministry of Health and Long Term Care. Ontario Drug Benefit Formulary, Number 37. March 7, 2001. www.gov.on.ca/health/english/program/drugs/odbf/odbf_mn.html Accessed on July 9, 2002.

Quebec Prescription Drug Insurance Plan. List of Medications. www.ramq.gouv.qc.ca/crc/eng/cit/assmed/cond.shtml Accessed on July 9, 2002.

Great Britain

British National Formulary (BNF). www.bnf.org Accessed on July 9, 2002.

National Institute for Clinical Excellence. Press Releases. www.nice.org.uk Accessed on July 9, 2002.

New Zealand

Medsafe. Consumer Medical Information. www.medsafe.govt.nz Accessed on July 9, 2002.

Pharmaceutical Management Agency (PHARMAC). New Zealand Pharmaceutical Schedule. www.pharmac.govt.nz Accessed on July 9, 2002.

United States

Food and Drug Administration (FDA). www.fda.gov Accessed on July 9, 2002.

FDA White Paper

Generic Drug Prices in the U.S. Are Lower Than Drug Prices in Canada

Office of Planning
November 2003

Advocates of legalizing imports of drugs from Canada and other countries have typically cited studies showing that brand-name drugs are much cheaper abroad than in the U.S. These studies ignore how competition in the U.S. market lowers generic drug prices so they are lower than drug prices abroad. In the U.S., generic drugs, which comprise roughly half of all prescriptions, are cheaper than both Canadian branded drugs and Canadian generic drugs. Low generic prices are fully compatible with strong incentives for R&D because generics are introduced in the U.S. only after patents expire.

For six of seven important generic drugs (alprazolam, clonazepam, enalapril, fluoxetine, lisinopril, metformin, and metoprolol), the U.S. generic was priced less than the brand name versions in Canada. Five of the seven U.S. generic drugs are cheaper than Canadian generics[i]. Of the remaining two generic drugs, while one (metformin) had a U.S. price 239 percent of the Canadian price, the other (enalapril) was unavailable in Canada generically. The price of the brand name version of enalapril in Canada was more than 5 times the price of the generic equivalent in the U.S.

These seven drugs are the biggest selling chronic-use drugs for which first US generic entry occurred in the last ten years. In particular, they are all the generic entities first entering the US market in the last ten years that are sold in solid dosage form, not over-the-counter, and are not anti-infectives. The prices represent the 2002 prices in U.S. dollars per milligram of active ingredient, calculated as average price of all milligrams sold in the respective countries. Prices in Canada were converted to prices in U.S. dollars using a 2002 exchange rate. The prices are retailer's acquisition costs and thus should predict retail prices to the extent that retail markups are the same in both countries.

The Canadian branded and generic prices relative to U.S. generic prices for these seven drugs appear in the figure below. Only one (metformin) sold for less in Canada either generically or as a brand name. Furthermore, metformin did not become available generically in the US until January 2002, so U.S. generic prices have likely not fallen to the level they will eventually reach.

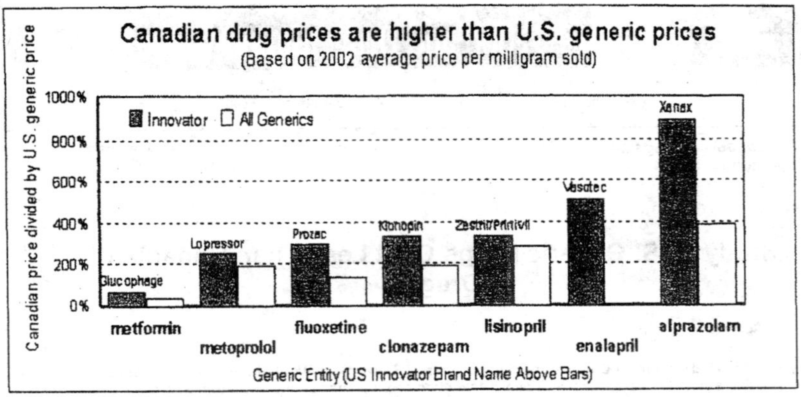

Data source: IMS Health, IMS National Sales Perspectives™

---

[i]For these analyses, the definition of a "generic" product differs from the IMS definition used in their MIDAS database. We defined three products types for each of the seven generic entities studied as follows:

1) Innovator product – any product marketed by the innovator of the generic entity. Xanax, for example, is the innovator product for alprazolam.

2) Branded Generic product – any product marketed by a multinational drug company (or it's subsidiary) other than the innovator product and sold under a trade name other than the products generic approved name. Clonapam, for example, marketed by ICN in Canada was considered a Branded Generic for these analyses.

3) Generic product – any product containing the generic entity, but not conforming to one of the two definitions above. For example, APO-Alpraz, Ratio-alprazolam and Nu-Alpraz were all considered generic products in Canada even though they sold under a name other than "alprazolam."

Thus, these analyses tend to contain relatively few "branded generic" products and relative many "generic" products compared to any analyses using the IMS MIDAS classifications.

FDA Consumer magazine
July-August 2004 Issue

Study: U.S. Generic Drugs Cost Less Than Canadian Drugs

By Linda Bren

If you think all drugs from Canada are cheaper than U.S. drugs, think again. In the United States, generic drugs--roughly half of all prescriptions--are often cheaper than both Canadian brand-name drugs and Canadian generic drugs, according to a study by the Food and Drug Administration.

FDA analysts looked at the seven biggest-selling generic prescription drugs for chronic conditions that became available as generics in the United States since 1993:

- alprazolam (generic for Xanax) for anxiety and panic disorders
- clonazepam (generic for Klonopin) for seizure and panic disorders
- enalapril (generic for Vasotec) for high blood pressure
- fluoxetine (generic for Prozac) for depression, obsessive-compulsive disorder, panic disorder, and bulimia nervosa
- lisinopril (generic for Zestril and Prinivil) for high blood pressure and heart failure
- metformin (generic for Glucophage) for type 2 diabetes
- metoprolol (generic for Lopressor) for high blood pressure, angina, and heart failure.

For six of the seven drugs, the U.S. generics were priced lower than the brand-name versions in Canada . Five of the seven U.S. generic drugs were also cheaper than the Canadian generics. Of the remaining two U.S. generic drugs, one (enalapril) was unavailable in Canada generically, and its Canadian brand-name version was more than five times the price of the U.S. generic equivalent. The other U.S. generic (metformin) sold for less in Canada both as a generic and as a brand name. Metformin did not become available generically in the United States until January 2002, so U.S. generic prices have likely not fallen to the level they will eventually reach, say the FDA Office of Planning economists who did the study.

The FDA study compared the average price of the generic and brand-name versions of seven drugs sold in the United States and Canada by calculating the price per milligram of active ingredients in U.S. dollars. Prices in Canada were converted to prices in U.S. dollars using a 2002 exchange rate. The prices were the costs to retailers, and should predict retail prices to the extent that retail markups are the same in both countries. Pricing information was collected by the pharmaceutical market research company IMS Health of Plymouth Meeting, Pa.

Advocates of legalizing imports of drugs from Canada and other countries have typically cited studies showing that brand-name drugs are much cheaper abroad than in the United States . These studies ignore how competition in the U.S. market lowers generic drug prices so they are lower than drug prices abroad, say FDA economists. U.S. generics have the same quality, safety, and strength as brand-name drugs, and they undergo the same rigorous review by the FDA before they are allowed on the market.

Drug standards and regulations differ from one country to another, and the FDA is responsible only for drugs that are sold within the United States . The agency is concerned about the strength, quality, and purity of medications that have not been approved for sale in the United States because they may not

have been manufactured under quality assurance procedures designed to make a safe and effective product.

"The standards for drug review and approval in the U.S. are the best in the world," says William Hubbard, FDA associate commissioner for policy and planning, "and the safety of our drug supply mirrors these high standards." But when U.S. consumers seek out Canadian suppliers, sources that purport to be Canadian, or other foreign sources that they believe to be reliable, they are taking a risk, he says. "While some foreign drug manufacturers submit their products to FDA for approval, the imported drugs arriving through the mail, through private express couriers, or by passengers arriving at ports of entry are often unapproved drugs that may not be subject to any reliable regulatory oversight. FDA cannot assure the safety of drugs purchased from such sources."

Verapamil SR 240mg (100)	High Blood Pressure	$83.90	$93.95	$43.97
Lisinopril 20mg (100)	High Blood Pressure	$83.59	$97.90	$16.19
Lisinopril 5mg (100)	High Blood Pressure	$47.96	$67.90	$13.99
Terazosin 2mg (100)	High Blood Pressure, Prostate	$43.98	$52.90	$17.09
Digitek 0.25mg (250)	Heart Medication	$51.30	N/A	$29.47
Diltiazem CD 240mg (100)	High Blood Pressure	$139.75	$145.00	$127.99
Hydrochlorothiazide 25mg (100)	High Blood Pressure	$12.73	N/A	$6.29
Warfarin 5mg (100)	Prevention of Blood Clotting	$18.60	$24.90	$20.69
Aricept 10mg (30)	Alzheimer's treatment	$128.65	$147.96	$140.69

*Shipping charges by Canadian pharmacies not included, but range from $15-$30.
**Based on prices available on Oct. 4 and 5, 2004.